The Elegant Taste of Thailand

Cha Am Cuisine

Cha-Am is a district town in Phetburi, an old province which has long played a prominent role in Thai history.

Phetburi was a center of civilization at an early date and at one time was the seat of kings. It has its own distinctive art and culture as well as the natural beauty of its hills and sea coasts. It is little wonder, then, that it is famed as a tourist destination. Among the local products are Phetburi rose apples, sugar, and a variety of sweets, among which **mo kaeng,** a type of custard, is perhaps the favorite.

Cha-Am itself is noted as a seaside resort. The reason is the long, clean beaches of fine, white sand and the magnificent expanse of tropical green sea lapping against them. The sunrises there are unforgettable. These attractions make Cha-Am a wonderful place to escape the heat and relax by the sea enjoyed by both Thais themselves and their guests from abroad.

The Elegant Taste of Thailand

Cha Am Cuisine

Second Edition

By

Pinyo Srisawat

&

Sisamon Kongpan

SLG BOOKS
Berkeley / Hong Kong

This Edition Published May 1998

SLG BOOKS
PO. Box 9465 Berkeley, CA 94709
Tel: (510) 525-1134
Fax: (510) 525-2632

First Published November 1989
Second Printing: September 1990
Third Printing: July 1991
Fourth Printing: October 1992
Fifth Printing: July 1993
Sixth Printing: April 1994
Seventh Printing: July 1995

Cover by Yuk Wah Lee
Editor: Roger Williams

Photographs by:
Sangwan Phrathep
Wisit Makham
Chaiyot Uluchada
Roger Williams

Typography: Mark Weiman/Regent Press

Color Separations and printing by
Snow Lion Graphics
Berkeley/Hong Kong

Library of Congress Cataloging-in-Publication Data

Pinyo Srisawat, 1956-
The elegant taste of Thailand / by Pinyo Srisawat & Sisamon Kongpon. – 2nd ed.
p/ cm.
Sisamon Kongpon's name appears first on the earlier edition.
Includes index.
ISBN 0-943389-23-2
1. Cookery, Thai. 2. Cookery — Thailand — Cha-am I. Sísamón Khongphan.
TX724.5.T5857 1998
641.59593 – de21 98-6961
CIP

CONTENTS

FOREWORD

When Pinyo, a.k.a. Jimmy, Srisawat first approached us to publish a Thai cookbook based on recipes from his very popular Thai restaurant Cha Am in Berkeley I had my reservations. Reservations, that is, aside from the almost weekly ones my partner and I had at his restaurant which just happened to be around the corner from our office in north Berkeley.

Three years, many recipe-testing meals and a lot of work later SLG Books published ***The Elegant Taste of Thailand***. With virtually no advertising and only a scattering of very good reviews the first printing of 10,000 books sold out in a few months. ***The Elegant Taste of Thailand*** has been back to press six times since its first printing. Its easy-to-follow, authentic recipes and superb color photographs made Thai cooking accessible to Western cooks of all levels.

While we were extremely pleased with our book's popularity in America we were ecstatic when it became a best seller in Thailand and a respected textbook at internationally known Thai cooking schools in Bangkok. Its availability in the Bangkok airport, Asia Books' bookstores and many of the better hotels in Thailand certainly helped introduce it to Asia travelers.

In the process of editing the English text of ***The Elegant Taste of Thailand*** a few helpful hints for the reader came to mind. I'd like to share these with you.

All transliteration can be somewhat confusing, all the more so if one does not speak the primary language involved. Different people, including professionals, will spell the same foreign word a variety of ways in English. Please don't allow these different renderings into English to annoy or confuse you. After all, an attempt is being made to reproduce words from Thai whose sounds do not exist in the English language. So when next you go to a Thai restaurant and see the word for chicken written as 'gai' and yet in this cook book it is written as 'kai', fear not, for it is the same word. Other examples follow: tod-thot, man-mun, kaeng-gaeng, rat-lad, pha naeng-panang, tom-dom, matsaman-mussaman, pet-ped and so on. I have seen tom yan kun, perhaps Thailand's most well known soup spelled at least a half a dozen similar but different ways.

As authenticity was the major impetus behind the creation of this Thai cookbook, we have retained the traditional ingredients as dictated by one of Thailand's foremost exponents in the field of Siamese culinary art. Therefore, if the recipe calls for fresh coriander (cilantro) root, then fresh coriander root it is. We apologize for any inconvenience this may cause our readers. We are certain the effort will result in a taste that will be more authentically Thai.

A good example would be the cucumber. When a particular recipe calls for 10 cucumbers, we mean "cucumber" as defined in the glossary , i.e. "short fruits about 8 cm (3 inches) long". Obviously we do not mean 10 cucumbers, 8 inches long, 5 inches in circumference, weighing 1/4 lb. each. You can substitute American or English cucumbers, but we ask you to take size and weight into consideration when you must implement substitutions.

The same can be said of celery. Chinese celery is much smaller and has a far stronger taste than Western celery. Therefore, when the recipe for Stuffed Cabbage instructs us to "Immerse the celery stalks in boiling water until flexible enough to be used for tying the cabbage leaves closed", we mean "celery stalks" as defined in our glossary.

What makes Thai food unique is the combination and balance of ingredients. If substitutions must be made, then we request that you be vigilant in your use of our thoroughly annotated and well-illustrated glossary.

It is our supreme desire that the recipes in ***The Elegant Taste of Thailand*** will satiate the palates of our most discerning Thai food fans. We are certain that the spectacular photographs of the beautifully presented dishes herein will titillate your appetite.

With this revised edition of ***The Elegant Taste of Thailand*** we again wish you good luck and good eating.

Roger Williams, Publisher
Berkeley, California
January, 1998

INTRODUCTION

Hey, you! You, there, with this book in your hands. There can be only two reasons your are reading these words:

1. You are standing in a bookstore trying to decide whether to invest the price of one great Thai dinner in order to get the clear instructions on how to make 100 great Thai dinners of your own.

To you, I have only one thing to say: waste not another minute, and get thee to the cash register. If you move quickly, you could actually be dining on Yam Sam Sahai (spicy pork, prawns, and chicken salad) this very evening. Check out the photo on page 76. If that doesn't inspire you to action, well all I can say is that I hope you enjoy your drive-thru burger with fries, you gastronomic heathen, you.

The hallmark of this book, and undoubtedly the reason the first edition went through seven good-sized printings and became a best-seller in Thailand itself, is that the recipes are quite wonderful, the instructions are clear and doable, the ingredients are readily available, the photos are both helpful and inspirational, and the results are spectacular.

2. Alternatively, you already own this book, and you needed something to read while you are waiting for your red mushroom curry (it's wonderful; it's on page 105) to cook. Let me help you while away the minutes (yes, as you doubtless already know, many recipes in this book are very fast indeed to prepare) by telling you the story of one of the reasons why this new and improved 2nd Edition did not reach the stores and your kitchen last year, instead of this year.

This splendid book had doubtless been delayed in part because this Introduction was late in coming. It was late in coming, because as I turned the pages of my advance copy, looking for inspiration, I came to the fateful page 179. I could go no further. A good recipe for Thai-style barbecued chicken had been one of the great quests of my life, ever since I first tasted this dish more than twenty years ago. The color photo gave me hope. The recipe was incredibly simple to follow. The end result was spectacular. The only small complaint was that line "Serves four to five," to which I can only say, "Hah! Maybe four or five ordinary hungry people, but nor yours truly after a five-mile hike in the hills."

Elsewhere, I have written that in my part of the world, Berkeley, California, during the early 1980s Thai restaurants seemed to spring from the earth like wildflowers in the spring. Although there was not a city law requiring at least one on every block, there were times it seemed that way. On a gastronomic scale of 0 to 10, they ranged from minus 1 on up to about, oh, say, 8 1/2. Truly, it was not until 1985, when Pinyo Srisawat opened his Cha Am restaurant in Berkeley, that my wife and I truly appreciated the heights to which Thai cuisine could rise, the perfect "seep," or "10" in Thai. We had not only come upon the Taj Mahal, but on the night of the full moon, with the string quartet softly playing Bach in the background.

If you're are fortunate enough to live within a day's sprint of one of the four Cha Am restaurants, then your are indeed blessed, and this book will serve well to help you reproduce some of the wonders you have been served there. And if you are one the 5,923,881,126 unfortunates who live outside Cha Am's primary customer zone, take heart. You will be able to recapture much of the essence of these world-class Thai restaurants right there in Wichita or Atlanta or wherever it is you live. But as you're simmering your Pha-naeng Neua (beef curried in sweet peanut sauce, page 111), do start thinking seriously about your first (or next) trip to Cha Am restaurants of Berkeley and San Francisco, the blessed source of the worthy inspirations for The Elegant Taste of Thailand.

John Bear
Berkeley, California
March, 1998

GLOSSARY

Agar-Agar, a thickening agent made from seaweed. Agar-agar is available in sheets of translucent strands or in a powder and can be found in most Asian markets and sometimes in health food stores.

Banana, *Nam Wa* variety, kluai nam wa, Musa sapientum, is probably the most popular eating banana among the nearly thirty varieties found in Thailand. It has short oblong fruits that become a pale yellow as they ripen. The leaf, bai tong, of this variety is used in Glutinous Rice Wrapped in Banana Leaf (page 213). Wrapping goes more easily if the sections are torn and allowed to stand overnight before wrapping.

Basil. There are many types of basil. The most commonly used basil in Thai cooking is sweet basil, horapha. It has deep green leaves and often reddish or purple stems. It has a taste reminiscent of anise and is especially good in curries. If you can not find horapha any basil can be substituted. Maenglak is another Thai sweet basil with light green leaves and a tangy taste.

Bay Leaf, *bai kra-wan*, is an elliptical leaf about 7 cm long, grey green on the bottom, having a brownish cast on the top, which is sold dried in the market.

Bean Curd, is made from soybeans that are soaked, ground, mixed with water and briefly cooked before being placed in a wooden mold to drain and solidify. There are several types of bean curd. Different types of dishes and different methods of cooking call for different types of bean curd. Soft white bean curd, tau hoo, is most often steamed or added to soups while the firm type, tao kwa, is used for stir-frying, deep frying and braising. Refrigerated bean curd will keep for about five days if the water is changed daily. Pressed and deep fried bean curd is also available. It can be found in dried cakes in most Asian markets.

Bean Curd, fermented, tau hoo yee, is more like cheese than tofu. It can be eaten with rice, used in cooking to enrich vegetable dishes or used as a seasoning. The two most common types are red fermented bean curd and white fermented bean curd. The red variety is cured in a brine with fermented red rice flavored with annatto seeds and rice wine.

Bean Curd, spongy. Deep-frying bean curd changes the texture into a sponge-like substance. This allows the bean curd to absorb the flavors of the sauce when it is cooked for a second time.

Bean Sauce, a seasoning made from fermented soybeans, flour and salt. This very popular Asian seasoning appears as yellow bean sauce, brown bean sauce, black bean sauce and hot bean sauce. The preferred sauce is made from whole beans as the ground varieties are often quite salty.

Beans, Black fermented, also known as salted black beans are cooked and fermented with salt and spices. These small, black, salted soy beans have a fantastic flavor when combined with garlic, fresh ginger, or chilies. Some chiefs soak the beans before use, others use directly from the container, crushing or chopping lightly to release the aroma.

Beans, Mung, *thua khiao*, are yellow beans with green shells. The shelled bean is used in sweets and the whole bean is sprouted, giving bean sprouts, thua ngok.

Beans, Winged, *thua phu*, bears a pod which in cross section looks like a rectangle that has a fringe-like extension at the corners: the "wings" of the bean.

Beans, Yard-long, *thua fak yao*, have pods up to 60 cm long. These are eaten both fresh and cooked and are at their best when young and slender.

Cabbage, Chinese, *phak kat khao*, Brassica campestris (pekinensis variety), has thin, light green leaves and broad, flat, thin ribs which form an elongated, rather than a spherical, head.

Cabbage, Swamp, *phak bung, Ipomoea aquatica*, also called water convolvulus, water spinach, or aquatic morning glory, has hollow stems and roughly triangular leaves. The Thai variety has delicate dark, green leaves and deep red stalks while the Chinese variety is thicker, larger, and lighter green. The tender tips of the stems are eaten fresh or cooked.

Cardamom, *luk kra-wan, Amomum krevanh*, appear like miniature unhusked coconuts. The pods and seeds are used in both sweet and savory dishes, especially curries. For best results grind the seeds just before using.

Celery, *kheun chai, Apium graveolens*, also called celeriac, turnip rooted celery or Chinese celery has very small stalks and a very strong flavor.

Cha Phlu, *Piper sarmentosum*, is a creeper with aromatic glossy dark green leaves which resemble those of the betel vine.

Chicken Stock, *nam sup*, made from fresh chicken is preferred in Thai cooking. While plain water can be substituted and the instant chicken broth cubes and pastes are certainly fast and convenient, they do not compare to home made stock. Chop 3 1/2 pounds of chicken bones and scraps into 3-4 inch pieces and place in a stock pot with 10 cups of water and allow to stand for 30 minutes. Peel 1 Chinese radish, cut in half length-wise and add to pot. Wash 3 celery plants and 3 garlic plants and remove the roots of the celery plants. Coil the celery and garlic plants together, tie into a bundle and add to the pot together with 5 bay leaves and 1 tablespoon salt. Heat to boiling, simmer over low heat for 1- 1 1/2 hours and then strain through cheesecloth.

Chilies, *phrik, Capsicum annum*, several varieties are available in Thailand. As they ripen they change color from green to red and become hotter. Removing the seeds and pulp from fresh chilies reduces their hotness. Fully ripe fruits are dried in the sun to give dried chilies, phrik haeng and these are pounded for ground dried chili, prik pon.

Chilies, Hot, *phrik khi nu*, are the hottest type and also the smallest, being only about a centimeter long. Generally the smaller the chili the hotter the flavor.

Chili Sauce, *phrik saus*, is made from water, chilies, salt, vinegar and sugar. The taste and degree of hotness or sweetness varies according to the brand. Many different brands from most Asian countries are available.

Chili Paste, *nam phrik phao*, see page 23

Chinese Chives, *ton kui chai*, Allium tuberosum, has fairly thick, narrow flat leaves which are eaten with fried noodle dishes such as Phat Thai, (see page 183).

Cilantro (see coriander)

Cinnamon, *op-choey, Cinnamonum spp.*, is the bark of a number of species of trees in this genus, classified in the laurel family. The types that grow in Southeast Asia are known commercially as cassias. The bark, which is generally reddish-brown, after being peeled from around the branch, tend to roll themselves back up, and so have a scroll-like appearance. For retail sale in Thai markets, the bark is cut into strips about 1 cm across and 8-10 cm long. Such strips are the basis for the measurements given in the recipes. Before use, the bark should be roasted to bring out its aroma

Cloves, *kan phlu*, are the very fragrant tack-like flower buds of the tree Caryophyllus aromaticus, thought to be native to insular Southeast Asia.

Coconut Milk, *ka-thi*, is the white liquid that is squeezed from grated coconut meat and not the juice inside the coconut. The use of coconut milk in curries is a hallmark of Thai cooking. To prepare about 1 1/2 cups coconut milk, add 2 cups fresh grated coconut to a food processor or blender. Add 1 1/4 cups very hot water and blend at high speed for one minute. Strain mixture through a fine sieve, pressing hard with a wooden spoon to extract as much liquid as possible. This is coconut milk. For recipes calling for thick coconut milk, allow the coconut milk to stand for a while, the thick milk will rise to the top. Spoon it off the top. The left over liquid will be light coconut milk. To prepare coconut milk from dried coconut flakes empty an 8-ounce package of unsweetened dried coconut flakes into a food processor. Add 1 7/8 cups of very hot, near boiling, water. Process with quick on and off pulses for 25 seconds or until well mixed. Strain the mixture through a fine sieve, pressing hard with a wooden spoon to extract as much liquid as possible. Canned coconut milk is very convenient and quite good. If a recipe calls for thick coconut milk, open the can and remove the thick milk that rises to the top. Use the contents just below the thick milk in recipes that call for light coconut milk. When the recipe calls for coconut milk, shake the can before opening.

Coriander seed
Pepper
Cumin seed
Star anise
Nutmeg
Cinnamon
Bay leaf
Kachai
Galangal

Chillies

Hot chillies

Dried chillies

Lime

Ginger

Shiitake mushroom

Cherry tomato

Lemon grass

Rice-straw mushroom

Coriander, *phak chi, Coriandrum sativum*, is of the parsley family. The leaves (referred to as cilantro in the text) and stems are eaten fresh and used frequently as a garnish. The root and the seeds are ingredients in many dishes. The root is taken from the fresh plant. The seeds which are roughly spherical and range in color from off-white to brown, have a pleasant taste and fragrance. It is better to roast and grind seeds immediately before use than to buy ground coriander seeds.

Corn Flour. What in many parts of Asia is called corn flour we call corn starch. So for the recipes in this cook book corn flour means corn starch.

Cucumber, Asian, *taeng kwa*, has short fruits about 3 inches long which are crispiest while still green and white, before yellowing. A larger type, taeng ran is also eaten, usually as a snack with chili and salt.

Cumin, *yi ra, Cuminium cyminum*, has elongated yellow-brown seeds about 5 mm in length. They should be dry roasted before use to heighten their fragrance.

Curry Powder, *phong ka-ri*, is a prepared mixture of spices such as turmeric, coriander seeds, ginger, cloves, cinnamon, mustard, cardamom, cumin, chili and salt. Each brand has its own character depending on the ingredients used.

Ear Fungus, *het hu nu*, is a dark grayish brown fungus that has a delightful crunchy texture. Soak in hot water for about 15 minutes and rinse well before use.

Eggplant, *ma kheua, Solanum spp.* In Thai cooking there are several types of eggplant aside from the more common long, thin lavender Chinese eggplant or the smaller nearly black Japanese eggplant. Ma kheua yao tastes very similar to Chinese and Japanese eggplant except they are green. These are served grilled, broiled or in curries. Ma kheua phung, Solanum torvum, grow in clusters and look like large peas. These miniature eggplants are slightly bitter but they nicely offset the rich taste of the curries in which they are used. Ma kheua pro is about the size of a ping pong ball. They can be white with a green cap, yellow-orange or purple in color. This eggplant is often eaten raw with a dipping sauce, or slightly cooked in a salads or curries.

Featherback, *pla krai*, is the freshwater fish Notopterus chitala

Fish, Dried, *pla haeng*, is a fresh water fish, such as serpent head, which is slit open, gutted, and spread to dry in the sun.

Fish, Salted, *pla khem*, is dried, salted sea fish, such as pla insee. In the market, the seller will cut you a steak of the required thickness. This is slowly roasted for a time to bring out the aroma

Fish Sauce, *nam pla*, is a clear brown liquid derived from a brew of fish or shrimp mixed with salt. It is sold in bottles and plastic jugs as well as in earthenware jars. High quality fish sauce has a fine aroma and taste. Fish sauce is placed on the table as a condiment at nearly every meal, either as is or mixed with sliced chilies and perhaps lime juice.

Five Spice Powder, *phong pha-loh*, is a prepared mixture of Sichuan peppercorns, fennel, clove, cinnamon, and star anise.

Galangal, *kha, Alpinia galangal*, is a larger and lighter colored relative of ginger and has its own distinctive flavor.

Garlic, *kra-thiam, Allium sativum*, is used both by the clove and by the entire bulb. The dry papery skin and the central core should be removed from bulbs. Cloves are often crushed by hitting with a spatula or the side of a knife blade and then the skins are picked out.

Garlic, Pickled, *kra-thiam dong*, are wonderfully flavorful and can be bought by the bulb or by the jar in the market

Garlic Plant, *ton kra-thiam, Allium sativum*, is the young plant picked before the bulb has formed. The leaves are flat and folded length-wise.

Ginger, *khing, Zingiber officinale*, grows from an underground stem, or rhizome. Mature ginger stems are buff colored. Young or fresh ginger, khing on, is white and is eaten fresh and pickled as well as cooked.

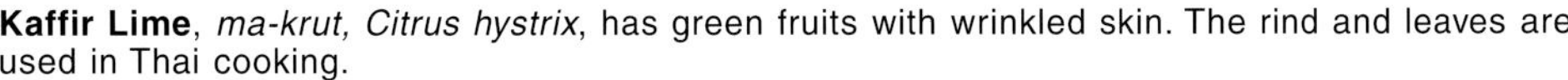

Kaffir Lime, *ma-krut, Citrus hystrix*, has green fruits with wrinkled skin. The rind and leaves are used in Thai cooking.

Kale, *phuk kha-na, Brassica oleracea (acephala* variety*)*, has leathery grey-green leaves on thick stalks. Stalk lovers buy the large variety, while those partial to the leaves get the dwarf variety.

Krachai, *Kaempferia panduratum*, sometimes known as lesser galangal grows in bunches of slender and short yellowish brown tuberous roots and is most often used in fish dishes.

Lemon Grass, *ta-khrai, Cymbopgon citratus*, is an aromatic green grass. The bases of the stems are used in cooking.

Lily Buds, *dok mai jeen, Hemerocallis spp*, are the dried unopened flowers of a type of day lily. The bright yellow buds will be fresher than the dark and brittle ones, which are old. Soak in hot water for 15-20 minutes or until soft. Cut off and discard the tough ends of the dried lily.

Mackerel, *pla thu*, is a small salt water fish, Rastrelliger chrysozonus (Scombridae). Steamed mackerel in small woven trays are sold in food shops nearly everywhere in the country.

Maggi Sauce is the brand name of a seasoning sauce that is made from water, corn gluten, soy protein and salt. It is used in many Thai recipes and should be available in most Asian markets.

Mungbeans, *thua khiao*, are yellow beans with green shells. The shelled bean is used in sweets and the whole bean is sprouted, giving bean sprouts, thua ngok.

Mushrooms, Cloud Ears, see Ear Fungus.

Mushrooms, Shiitake, *het hom, Lentinus edodes*, often called Japanese dried mushrooms. The Japanese cultivate them on the shii tree, thus the name shiitake, (take is Japanese for mushroom). The Chinese have been gathering them for over a thousand years and prefer them dried to fresh. The best tasting and most expensive mushrooms are the large, thick, light brown ones with a cracked surface, but all grades add flavor and aroma to any recipe.

Mushrooms, Straw, *het fang*, used in soups, salads and curries. Straw mushrooms have a sweet and nutty flavor and although they are available canned we suggest you substitute a fresh alternative such as oyster mushrooms.

Mustard Greens, Chinese, *phak kwang tung*, Brassica campestris (chinensis variety), has dark oval leaves on thick fleshy stalks.

Noodles, Egg, *ba mi*, are yellow noodles made from wheat flour and eggs. Small balls of this kind of noodle are available in the market.

Noodles, Mungbean, *wun sen*, are thread-like noodles made from mung bean flour. They are sold dried and are soaked in water before use. When cooked they become transparent. High quality noodles maintain their integrity in soup better than do cheap ones.

Noodles, Rice, *kuai-tiao*, are flat white noodles made from rice flour. Uncut fresh noodle sheets are sold in the market. They are also sold in three widths: wide, sen yai (2-3 cm), narrow, sen lek (5 mm) and thin, sen mi (1-2 mm). Dried noodles are soaked in water before use to soften them.

Noodles, Vermicelli, *khanom jin*, are thin round noodles, made from either wheat or rice flour. Fresh vermicelli are sold in the form of wads that look like birds nests.

Onion, *hom hua yai, Allium cepa*, has light colored bulbs that are larger and milder that those of the shallot.

Onion, Spring, *ton hom, Allium fistulosum*, also called spring onions or scallions, has leaves that are circular in cross-section. These are much used as a garnish. The bulbs are frequently served on the side of one-dish meals, such as fried rice, or placed on a salad plate.

Baby corn
Sponge gourd
Wax gourd
Chinese cabbage
Yard-long bean
Long eggplant
Celery
Swamp cabbage

Sweet basil *(maeng lak)*

Spring onion

Chinese chive

Coconut

Garlic plant

Mint

Ma-kheua phuang

Ma-kheua pro

Sweet basil *(horapha)*

Coriander

Oyster Sauce, *nam man hoi*, is a rich, viscous seasoning sauce made from fresh oysters, salt and spices. A wonderful and popular seasoning for seafood, meat and poultry. It is especially good over stir fried vegetables such as kai lan, bok choy and choy sam.

Palm Sugar, *nam tan pep*, was originally made from the sap of the sugar Palmyra palm, *Borassus flabellifera*, called tan in Thai, which has a very rough trunk and large, fan-shaped leaves. Now it is generally made from the sap of the coconut palms and may be sold as coconut sugar. The sugar is a light golden brown paste with a distinctive flavor and frangrance.

Peppercorns, *phrik thai, piper nigrum*, produces berries, which when ripe, are dried and ground with the skins on to give black pepper, or with the skins removed to give white pepper. The most widely available form in Thailand is white pepper.

Pickled Plum, *buai dong*, is the preserved fruit of an oriental plum which is sometimes labeled Japanese apricot.

Pork Belly, *mu sam chan*, is bacon-cut pork, with layers of red meat, fat and skin.

Prawns, Dried, *kung haeng*, are small shrimp which have been dried in the sun. Look for the bright orange ones as they are the best. Dried shrimps should be soaked in hot water or rice wine before use. The soaking liquid can also be used.

Radish, Chinese, *hua phak*, hus chai hao, Raphanus sativus, (longpinnatus variety), has a long, cylindrical root that looks like a hefty, white carrot.

Radish, Preserved, sometimes called salted turnip, is available in Asian markets. It should be washed before use.

Rice, *khao jao*, the staple food in the central and southern parts of Thailand, is long-grained, non-glutinous rice. Uncooked grains are translucent. When cooked, the rice is white and fluffy.

Rice, Fermented, *khao niao*, is made by fermenting cooked glutinous rice and is sold as a sweet.

Rice, Glutinous, *khao niao*, also known as sticky rice, is the mainstay of the diet in the northern and northeastern regions of the country and is used in confections in all regions. Uncooked grains are starchy white in color.

Rice Flour, *paeng khao jao*, is made from non-glutinous rice.

Rice Flour, Glutinous, *paeng khao niao*, is made from glutinous rice.

Rice Paper, made from a mixture of rice flour, water and salt. Rice paper needs to be softened before use. Carefully dip one or two sheets in a warm sugar-water solution and soak until soft, a minute or two. Drain on a towel before rolling. Look for white rice papers. Stay away from packages with broken pieces and yellowish papers.

Rice Wine, brewed from glutinous rice. Use Chinese Shaoxing rice wine for the recipes in this book (A good, dry pale sherry can be substituted). Japanese rice wine, sake, is quite different and should not be used.

Rock Cod, *pla kao*, is also known as grouper, reef cod, and sea bass.

Sago, a starchy foodstuff derived from the soft interior of the trunk of various palms and cycads, used in making puddings.

Sea Perch, *pla kaphong*, is a general name for fish of the sea bass and sea perch families.

Serpent Head, *pla chon*, is the freshwater fish Ophiocephalus striatus.

Sesame, *nga*, Sasamum indium, has small oval seeds which are white and have dark hulls. They are usually sold hulled.

Shallots, *hom lek or hom daeng, Allium ascalonicum*, is the zesty small red onion favored in Thai cooking.

Shrimp Paste, *ka-pi*, is shrimp which are salted, fermented for a time, allowed to dry in the sun then ground and worked with the addition of moisture into a fine-textured paste, which is fragrant and slightly salty. A little bit goes a long way for the Western palate.

Sichuan Pepper, *Zanthoxylum simulans*, also known as Chinese pepper, (except in China where it is called flower pepper) are a reddish-brown color with a pungent aroma and astringent flavor.

Soy Sauce, *si iu*, used in these recipes is the Chinese rather than the Japanese type. Soy sauce is prepared from a mixture of soybeans, flour and water, which is fermented and aged. The three most commonly used soy sauces are light soy sauce (si iu khao), dark soy sauce (si iu dam) and mushroom soy sauce. Light soy sauce can be substituted as a vegetarian alternative to fish sauce. Dark soy sauce is aged longer than light soy sauce and is slightly thicker, sweeter and stronger although light soy sauce is usually saltier. The dark soy sauce is preferable for dipping while the light soy sauce is most often used in cooking. Mushroom soy sauce is infused with straw mushrooms and imparts a delicious flavor.

Sponge Gourd, *buap liam, Luffa acutangula*, also called vegetable gourd or Chinese okra, is oblong, pointed, and dark green and has sharp longitudinal ridges.

Star Anise, *poi kak bua, Illicium verum*, a small, dried, dark brown, star-shaped spice with many pods. Star anise has a pungent licorice flavor. When a recipe calls for one whole star anise, it means eight individual pods. Buy star anise whole and not broken in pieces. It is most often used in braised dishes to which it imparts a rich taste and delightful fragrance.

Sugar, *nam tan sai*, is granulated cane sugar. Colors range from white to reddish and textures from fine to coarse. Some people find the reddish sugar tastier than the more highly refined white.

Tamarind, *ma-kham*, Tamarindus indica, is a tree which bears tan pods inside of which are bean-like hard brown seeds surrounded by sticky flesh. The tan pod shell can be easily removed. Ripe tamarind, ma-kham piak, is the flesh, seeds, and veins, of several fruits pressed together in the hand to form a wad. The immature fruit, the young leaves and the flowers are also used, all to give a sour taste.

Tamarind Juice, *nam som ma-kham*, is obtained by mixing some of the ripe fruit with water and squeezing out the juice.

Tapioca Pellets, *sa-khu met lek*, are tiny balls (about 2 mm in diameter) made from tapioca (cassava tubers), used in some sweets. They should be mixed with hot, but not scalding, water and kneaded, and allowed to stand for a time covered with a damp cloth to permit the water to penetrate to the core.

Tapioca Flour, *paeng man sampalang*, is made from tapioca, or cassava tubers. When this or any of other flour is used to thicken a sauce it is first mixed with a little water so it will not lump in the sauce.

Taro Root, *Colocasia esculenta*, is actually a rhizome roughly spherical, covered with a rough skin with a whitish flesh, sometimes spotted with purple. It was used as a source for starch before rice was the everyday stable. Taro is sweet, starchy and doughy in texture. It can be eaten as dessert, a deep-fried snack or substituted for potatoes in a main dish. In Hawaii taro is used to make poi.

Tofu, see bean curd.

Turmeric, *kha-min, Curcuma longa*, is a small ginger with brown rhizomes. Inside the flesh is a bright carrot orange. Also used as a coloring agent.

Water Chestnut, *haeo*, is the tuber of certain kinds of sedges. The skin is dark and the crunchy meat inside is off-white.

Wax Gourd, *fak khiao*, Benincasa hispida, also called white gourd or Chinese preserving melon, is oblong and light green to white. The ends are rounded and the flesh is solid and white.

Won Ton Skins, it is no longer necessary to make these by hand. Very good commercially made wrappers are available at most markets. Buy the very thin ones if possible. They freeze very well, so you can use what you need and wrap the unused wrappers well before freezing.

NAM PHRIK PHAO
(Roasted Chili Sauce)

INGREDIENTS :

1/2	cup small dried chillies
3	tbsp. fish sauce
2	cups vegetable oil
1/3	tsp. salt
8	shallots, sliced
6	garlic cloves, sliced
1	cup dried shrimp
1	tbsp. palm sugar
1 1/2	tbsp. tamarind juce

PREPARATION:

- ■ Heat the oil in a wok and fry the shallots and garlic until golden brown; remove from oil and drain. Add the dried shrimp and dried chillies; fry until golden brown; remove from oil and drain.
- ■ In a mortar or blender, grind the shrimp, garlic, chillies, shallots and sugar until the mixture is blended well. Add the fish sauce, tamarind juice, salt and cooled oil from the wok into the blender; blend until you have a finely textured sauce.
- ■ This can be stored in a glass jar in the refrigerator for about 3-4 months.

Nam Phrik Kaeng Matsaman
(Massaman Curry Paste)

INGREDIENTS :

3	dried chillies, soaked in hot water for 15 minutes and deseeded
3	tbsp. chopped shallots
2	tbsp. chopped garlic
1	tsp. chopped galangal
1 1/4	tbsp. chopped lemon grass
2	cloves
1	tbsp. coriander seeds
1	tsp. cumin seeds
5	pepper corns
1	tsp. shrimp paste
1	tsp. salt

PREPARATION:

- ■ In a wok over low heat put the shallots, garlic, galangal, lemon grass, cloves, coriander seeds, cumin seeds and dry fry for about 5 minutes, then grind into a powder.
- ■ Into a blender, put the rest of the ingredients except the shrimp paste and blend to mix well. Add the shallot-garlic-galangal-lemon grass-clove-coriander seed-cumin seed mixture and the shrimp paste and blend again to obtain 1/2 cup of a fine-textured paste.
- ■ This can be stored in a glass jar in the refrigerator for about 3-4 months.

Nam Phrik Kaeng Ka-ri

(Yellow Curry Paste)

INGREDIENTS :

3	dried chillies, soaked in hot water for 15 minutes and deseeded
3	tbsp. chopped shallots
1	tbsp. chopped garlic
1	tsp. chopped ginger
1	tbsp. coriander seeds
1	tsp. cumin seeds
1	tbsp. chopped lemon grass
1	tsp. shrimp paste
1	tsp. salt
2	tsp. curry powder

PREPARATION:

- In a wok over low heat, put the shallots, garlic, ginger, coriander seeds and cumin seeds and dry fry for about 5 minutes, then grind into a powder.
- Into a blender, put the rest of the ingredients and blend to mix well. Add the shallot-garlic-ginger-coriander seed-cumin seed mixture and blend again to obtain about 1/2 cup of a fine-textured paste.
- This can be stored in a glass jar in the refrigerator for about 3-4 months.

Nam Phrik Kaeng Khua

(Kaeng Khua Curry Paste)

INGREDIENTS :

5	dried chillies, soaked in hot water for 15 minutes and deseeded
3	tbsp. chopped shallots
2	tbsp. chopped garlic
1	tsp. chopped galangal
1	tbsp. chopped lemon grass
1	tsp. chopped kaffir lime rind
1	tsp. chopped coriander root
2	tsp. salt
1	tsp. shrimp paste

PREPARATION:

- Into a blender, put all ingredients except the shrimp paste and blend until well mixed. Then, add the shrimp paste and blend once more to obtain about 3/4 cup of a fine-textured paste.
- This can be stored in a glass jar in the refrigerator for about 3-4 months.

Nam Phrik Kaeng Khiao Wan

(Green Curry Paste)

INGREDIENTS :

15	green hot chillies
3	tbsp. chopped shallots
1	tbsp. chopped garlic
1	tsp. chopped galangal
1	tbsp. chopped lemon grass
1/2	tsp. chopped kaffir lime rind
1	tsp. chopped coriander root
5	pepper corns
1	tbsp. coriander seeds
1	tsp. cumin seeds
1	tsp. salt
1	tsp. shrimp paste

PREPARATION:

- In a wok over low heat, put the coriander seeds, and cumin seeds and dry fry for about 5 minutes, then grind into a powder.
- Into a blender, put the rest of the ingredients except the shrimp paste and blend to mix well. Add the coriander-cumin seed mixture and the shrimp paste and blend to obtain 1/2 cup of a fine-textured paste.
- This can be stored in a glass jar in the refrigerator for about 3-4 months.

Nam Phrik Kaeng Som

(Sour Soup Curry Paste)

INGREDIENTS :

7	dried chillies, soaked in hot water for 15 minutes and deseeded
3	tbsp. chopped shallots
1	tbsp. chopped garlic
2	tbsp. chopped krachai
1	tbsp. shrimp paste
1	tsp. salt

PREPARATION:

- Into a blender, put all ingredients except the shrimp paste and blend until mixed well. Then, add the shrimp paste and blend once more to obtain about 1/2 cup of a fine-textured paste.
- This can be stored in a glass jar in the refrigerator for about 3-4 months.

Nam Phrik Kaeng Daeng
(Red Curry Paste)

INGREDIENTS :

13	small dried chillies, soaked in hot water for 15 minutes and deseeded
3	tbsp. chopped shallot
4	tbsp. chopped garlic
1	tbsp. chopped galangal
2	tbsp. chopped lemon grass
2	tsp. chopped kaffir lime rind
1	tbsp. chopped coriander root
20	pepper corns
1	tsp. shrimp paste
1	tbsp. coriander seed
1	tsp. cumin seed

PREPARATION:

- In a wok over low heat, put the coriander seeds and cumin seeds and dry fry for about 5 minutes, then grind into a powder.
- Into a blender, put the rest of the ingredients except the shrimp paste and blend to mix well. Then add the coriander seed-cumin seed mixture and the shrimp paste and blend again to obtain about 3/4 cup of a fine-textured paste.
- This can be stored in a glass jar in the refrigerator for about 3-4 months.

Po-Pia Thot

(Egg Rolls)

INGREDIENTS :

1	pack egg-roll sheets
1/2	lb. ground pork
3	oz. crab meat
1	egg
1	3-oz. pack mungbean noodles
1/2	cup shredded carrot
1/2	cup shredded cabbage
1/3	cup (5-6) dried ear mushrooms, chopped (soaked in hot water)
1/2	tbsp. black pepper
1	tbsp. chopped garlic
1/2	tsp. salt
1	tbsp. light soy sauce
3	cups cooking oil

Paste made by mixing 2 tbsp. wheat flour in 1/4 cup water and stirring over low heat.

PREPARATION:

- Soak the noodles until soft, then cut into short lengths.
- Mix pork, egg, cabbage, carrots, mushrooms, pepper and light soy sauce together then add the noodles and mix well.
- Fry the garlic in 3 tbsp. oil and then add the pork and noodle mixture. Fry until fairly dry, then set aside to cool.
- Place a teaspoonful of the filling on an egg roll sheet, fold the sheet over the filling, fold about half a turn, fold in the ends to close them; then, roll up tightly, sealing the sheet closed with the paste.
- Deep fry in plenty of oil over low heat until crisp and golden brown.
- Serve with sauce, sliced cucumber, and sweet basil leaves.

INGREDIENTS FOR EGG ROLL SAUCE :

1/4	cup vinegar
1/4	cup water
1/2	cup sugar
1/2	tsp. salt
1/2	tbsp. chilli, well pounded
2	tsp. tapioca flour mixed in 2 tbsp. water

PREPARATION:

- Mix the vinegar, water, sugar, salt and chilli; heat to boiling, add a little of the flour water, boil a short time, then remove from heat.

Thot Man
(Fish Cakes)

INGREDIENTS :

1 1/2	lb. white fish meat (e.g. ladyfinger), minced or chopped
1	tbsp. red curry paste (see page 26)
1	egg
1/2	cup yard-long beans, minced or chopped
1/3	cup kaffir lime leaves, minced or chopped
1/2	tsp. salt
2	tsp. sugar
3	cups vegetable oil

PREPARATION:

- Put all the ingredients into a large bowl and mix well with the hand.
- Shape into small patties about 3" in diameter and deep fry in vegetable oil until golden brown.
- Serve with peanut sweet chilli sauce.

Peanut Sweet Chilli Sauce

- Use cucumber relish (see p. 37) and add 1/4 cup sliced shallots and 1/2 cup freshly ground peanuts.
- Serves four.

Pik Kai Thot

(Fried Stuffed Chicken Wings)

INGREDIENTS :

1	cup breadcrumbs
6	chicken wings, deboned
1	cup mungbean noodles, soaked in warm water for 15 minutes and then cut into 1/2″ pieces
1	tbsp. chopped coriander greens
1/2	cup sliced water chestnuts
2	eggs
1	tbsp. chopped garlic
1/3	cup wheat flour
1/2	lb. ground pork

PREPARATION:

- Mix together the noodles, coriander, chestnuts, one egg, garlic, flour and ground pork and stuff this mixture into the deboned chicken wings (see p. 22) (not too full).
- Steam the chicken wings for 15 minutes; then, drain and cool. Mix one egg with the breadcrumbs and dip the chicken wings into this mixture and deep fry them until golden brown.
- Slice and serve with sweet chilli sauce. (See p. 179)
- Serves four to six.

Mu reu Neua Sa-te

(Pork or Beef Sateh)

INGREDIENTS :

1	lb. pork (or beef)
2	tsp. ground roasted coriander seeds
1/2	tsp. ground roasted cumin seeds
1	tsp. finely chopped galangal
1	heaping tbsp. finely chopped lemon grass
1	tsp. finely chopped turmeric
1/4	tsp. ground pepper
1	tsp. salt
2	tsp. sugar
1/2	cup coconut milk
	bamboo skewers

PREPARATION:

- Cut the meat into thin slices about 1 inch wide and 2 inches long.
- Pound the coriander seeds, cumin, galangal, lemon grass, tumeric, salt, and pepper in a mortar until finely ground. Pour over the meat along with the sugar and the coconut milk, mix thoroughly, and set aside to marinate for 30 minutes.
- Skewer the meat strips lengthwise and broil over a medium charcoal fire, brushing occasionally with the remaining marinade. Serve with sauce and relish.
- Serves four.

Sateh Sauce

INGREDIENTS :

1/4	cup red curry paste (see page 26)
2	cups coconut milk
1/2	cup creamy peanut butter
1/4	cup sugar
1/4	cup tamarind juice
salt	

Sateh Sauce
(Continued)

PREPARATION:

- Mix the peanut butter and the red curry paste together well.
- Skim one cup of coconut cream from the coconut milk. Heat the coconut cream in a wok until the oil surfaces; then, add the peanut butter-curry paste mixture and stir to mix well. Add the remaining coconut milk and reduce the heat. Continue to stir regularly.
- Season to taste with sugar and tamarind juice, and if you like, with salt. When the sauce has thickened, pour into a serving bowl.

Cucumber Relish

INGREDIENTS :

4	cucumbers (see page 21)
2	shallots
1	chilli
1/3	cup vinegar
2	tsp. sugar
1	tsp. salt

PREPARATION:

- Wash and peel the cucumbers, cut in half lengthwise, and then cut across into thin slices. Cut the shallots and chillies into thin slices. Place the cucumber, shallot, and chilli slices in a bowl.
- Heat the vinegar, sugar, and salt, stirring constantly until sugar has dissolved. When the mixture comes to a boil, remove from the heat. After the mixture has cooled, add it to the bowl and garnish with chopped coriander greens.
- Serves four.

Mu Pan Kon Thot

(Fried Pork Meatballs)

INGREDIENTS :

2	cups ground pork
1	tbsp. well pounded garlic
1	tsp. salt
1	tbsp. fish sauce
2	tbsp. water
1/2	tsp. pepper
2	tsp. well pounded coriander root
1	cup cooking oil

PREPARATION:

- Mix the pork, salt, fish sauce, pepper, garlic, and coriander root together.
- Take portions of the mixture of about one tablespoon and form into meatballs.
- Place the oil in a wok on medium heat. When the oil is hot, fry the meatballs until golden brown; remove and drain.
- Serve with pineapple, tomato, and spring onions.
- Serves four.

Thot Man Khao Phot

(Fried Sweet Corn Patties)

INGREDIENTS :

2	cups sweet corn kernels
1/4	tsp. pepper
1	tsp. salt
2	tsp. well-pounded garlic
2	tsp. wheat flour
1	egg
2	cups cooking oil

PREPARATION:

- Knead together well the corn, pepper, salt, garlic, egg, and flour to obtain a stiff dough.
- Place the oil in a deep wok over medium heat. When the oil is hot, pick up about 1 tbsp. of the dough, shape into a patty with the fingers, and place the patty in the oil. Continue making patties and putting them in but do not crowd the wok. Turn as needed so the patties brown on both side; then, remove from the oil and drain on absorbent paper.
- Serve with chilli sauce.
- Serves four.

Khanom Pang Na Kung Roi Nga

(Fried Canapés with Prawn Spread)

INGREDIENTS :

8 slices bread
1 oz. prawns
4 oz. lean pork
1 egg
1 tsp. thinly sliced coriander root
5 cloves garlic
1/8 tsp. pepper
2 tsp. light soy sauce
1/4 tsp. salt
2 tbsp. white sesame seeds
3 cups cooking oil

PREPARATION:

- Dry the bread in a low temperature oven. Alternatively, use bread which has dried out, for this will absorb less oil and give you very crisp canapés.
- Shell and clean the prawns, add the pork, and mince.
- Remove the skins of the garlic cloves, place in a mortar with the coriander root and pepper, and pound to a fine paste.
- Knead the pounded garlic mixture together with the minced pork and prawn; then, add the egg and knead once again until uniform in consistency.
- Divide the mixture into eight portions and spread one portion on each slice of bread. Smooth the surface of the spread and sprinkle with about 1/2 tsp. seasame seeds.
- Heat the oil in a deep wok. When it is hot, fry each slice of bread spread-side down. When the spread has become golden brown, remove the bread from the oil and drain on absorbent paper.
- Cut each slice of bread into quarters, arrange on a serving platter, and seve with marmalade sauce or maggi sauce and fresh vegetables, such as chilled cucumber discs, or pickled ginger.

INGREDIENTS :

1/4 cup marmalade
1/4 cup vinegar
1/4 tsp. salt

PREPARATION:

- Mix the ingredients in a pot, heat, stirring just long enough to mix together well, and then transfer to a bowl.
- Serves four.

Khanom Pang Na Mu

(Fried Canapés with Pork Spread)

INGREDIENTS :

1 1/2	cups ground pork
1	beaten egg
2	tbsp. water
1	tbsp. light soy sauce
1	tsp. finely chopped coriander root
1/2	tsp. pepper
5	cloves garlic
10	slices bread
1	finely sliced red chilli
4	cups cooking oil
1/4	cup chopped fresh coriander

PREPARATION:

- Blend the pork with half of the egg. Pound the coriander root, pepper, and garlic well in a mortar and then knead into the pork mixture, adding the water.
- Cut the slices of bread into quarters; these may be either square or triangular. Dry the bread by heating in a low temperature oven. Place about 1 tbsp. of the pork spread on each piece of bread and spread it so that it mounds in the center and slopes smoothly right to the edges. Smear the spread with some of the remaining egg and decorate with coriander greens and slices of red chilli.
- Heat the oil in a wok. When it is hot, fry the pieces of bread spread-side downward until golden brown; then, remove from the oil and drain.
- Serve with slices of fresh cucumber or with cucumber relish.
- Serves four to six.

Mi Krop

(Crispy Candied Noodles)

INGREDIENTS :

5	oz. thin rice noodles
1/4	cup finely chopped fresh shrimp
1/4	cup finely chopped pork
1	cake yellowbeancurd, cut into matchstick-size pieces and fried crisp
1	tbsp. chopped garlic and shallot
1	tbsp. fermented soybeans
1	tbsp. vinegar
1	tbsp. fish sauce
4	tbsp. palm sugar
1	tbsp. lime juice
1	tsp. ground dried chillies
2	oz. bean sprouts
3	Chinese chives (gao choy)
1	chilli, thinly sliced
1	coriander plant
2	pickled garlic bulbs, thinly sliced
3	cups cooking oil

PREPARATION:

- If the noodles are very fine, fry in oil until crisp and golden brown, then drain. If the noodles are thick, soak 15 minutes in water, drain well, and then fry a few at a time.
- Heat 1/4 cup oil in a frying pan. Fry the garlic and shallots until fragrant, then add the pork and shrimp, seasoning with fermented soybeans, vinegar, fish sauce, sugar and dried chilllies. When thick, add the lime juice. Mix and season to obtain a sweet, sour, and salty flavor.
- Reduce the heat, add the noodles and continue stirring in the sauce until they stick together; then, add the beancurd; mix and spoon onto plates.
- Sprinkle with the pickled garlic, finely sliced kaffir lime rind, coriander, and chilli. Place bean sprouts and Chinese chives along the sides of the plates.
- Serves four.

Khao Tang Na Tang

(Fried Potcrust and Dip)

INGREDIENTS FOR FRIED POTCRUST :

1	lb. rice-pot crust
4	cups cooking oil

PREPARATION:

- Place the oil in a deep wok over medium heat. When the oil is hot, fry the potcrust a few pieces at a time, turning as necessary until golden brown on both sides; then, remove from the oil and drain.

  bread can also be fried crisp in this way.

INGREDIENTS FOR DIP :

1/2	cup minced pork
1/2	cup minced prawn (about 7 oz. fresh prawns)
1/4	cup ground roasted peanuts
1 3/4	cups coconut milk
1	dried chilli, seeds removed and soaked in water
1	tsp. sliced coriander root
1/4	tsp. pepper
4	cloves garlic
2	tbsp. sugar
1-2	tbsp. fish sauce
1	tbsp. thinly sliced shallot
1	tbsp. chopped fresh corainder

PREPARATION:

- Pound the coriander root, pepper, chilli, and garlic well in a mortar.
- Bring the coconut milk to a boil in a wok. When some oil has surfaced, add the coriander root-pepper-garlic mixture and stir to disperse. Next, add the prawns and pork, stir well and season to taste with the sugar and fish sauce. When the dip has come to a boil once again, add the peanuts and shallots, remove from heat, and sprinkle with a little chopped fresh coriander.
- Serve with fried potcrust, crisp fried bread, or melba toast.
- Serves three to four.

Nam Phrik Ong

(Pork and Tomato Chilli Dip)

INGREDIENTS :

5	dried chillies, soaked
1	tbsp. finely sliced galangal
3	tbsp. chopped onion
5	cloves garlic (whole)
1	tsp. salt
1	tsp. shrimp paste
3	tbsp. chopped pork
1	cup cherry tomatoes
3	cloves garlic, chopped
1	coriander plant
2	tbsp. cooking oil
1/2	cup water

Fresh Vegetables :
cucumber, yard-long beans, winged beans
Boiled Vegetables :
yard-long beans, eggplant, pumpkin vine tips, swamp cabbage, banana blossom

PREPARATION:

- Pound the chillies, salt, and galangal well in a mortar. Add the onion, shrimp paste, and the five garlic cloves and pound to mix thoroughly. Add the pork and continue pounding to mix. Finally, add the tomatoes and pound to mix well.
- Heat the oil in a wok. When it is hot, add the chopped garlic. When the garlic is fragrant, add the pork and tomato chili paste and continue frying over low heat stirring until the ingredients take on a gloss; then, add the water.
- Continue cooking with regular stirring until much of the water evaporates and the mixture becomes fairly thick. Then, transfer to a bowl, sprinkle with chopped coriander, and serve with fresh vegetables, boiled vegetables or both.
- Serves four.

Lon Tao Jiao

(Coconut Milk and Fermented Soybean Dip)

INGREDIENTS :

1	lb. grated coconut or 1 1/2 cups coconut milk
1/2	cup fermented soybean
3	tbsp. chopped shrimp
3	tbsp. chopped pork
4	shallots
3-5	chillies
3	tbsp. sugar
3	tbsp. tamarind juice

PREPARATION:

- Add 3/4 cup warm water to the coconut and squeeze out 1 1/2 cups coconut milk.
- Heat the coconut milk in wok until oil comes to the surface.
- Strain the fermented soybean, place the solids in a mortar with 2 shallots and pound until mixed thoroughly. Mix with coconut milk in the wok over low heat. Add the shrimp, pork, and chillies and cook over low heat until done. Add 2 sliced shallots, sugar and tamarine juice to taste, bring to a boil and remove from heat.
- Serve with fresh vegetables, such as cabbage, cucumbers, and coriander.
- Serves four.

Kalampli Phan Tao Hu
(Stuffed Cabbage)

INGREDIENTS :

8	good-sized cabbage leaves
1	tsp. salt
2	Chinese celery plants or 8 cocktail toothpicks (see page 20)
3	cakes soft white bean curd
1/4	cup finely chopped garlic plant
1/2	lb. ground pork
2 1/2	tbsp. sugar
5	tbsp. ligth soy sauce
1	egg
2	cups chicken stock
1	tbsp. corn flour

thin slices of lime

PREPARATION:

■ Wash the cabbage leaves well, taking care not to tear them. Immerse the leaves in boiling water to which salt has been added. When the leaves have become flexible enough to be used for wrapping, remove from the water.

■ Wash the celery, remove the roots and leaves, and immerse the stalks in boiling water until flexible enough to be used for tying the cabbage leaves closed.

■ In a wok over low heat, fry the pork and garlic plant, breaking up the pork into small bits and adding 1/2 tbsp. sugar and 1 tbsp. light soy sauce. When the pork is done, add the bean curd, again breaking it up into small bits. Then, reduce the heat, add the egg, and stir to mix thoroughly.

■ Divide the filling into eight portions, placing each in the middle of a cabbage leaf. Fold two opposite sides over the filling, roll up tightly, and tie with celery stalks, or pin closed with toothpicks.

■ Arrange the stuffed cabbage leaves in wok, add the chicken stock and the remaining light soy sauce and sugar, and simmer for about 20 minutes.

■ Mix the corn flour with 2 tbsp. water to obtain a smooth batter, pour this into the wok, reduce the heat, and allow the sauce to thicken.

■ Arrange the stuffed cabbage leaves on a serving plate, pour the sauce over them, and place lime slices on top.

■ Serves four.

Kaeng Som Cha-Am

(Cha- Am Sour Tamarind Soup)

INGREDIENTS FOR SPICE MIXTURE :

3	small dried red chilies
1	tsp. salt
1 1/2	tsp. chopped fresh lemon grass
2	medium-sized shallots
1	tsp. shrimp paste

OTHER INGREDEINTS :

1 1/2	lbs. medium-sized prawns shelled and deveined or sea perch
2	lbs. fresh green vegetables (e.g., yard-long beans, cabbage, cauliflower, Chinese cabbage)
4 1/2	cups chicken stock or water
4	tbsp. fish sauce
2	tbsp. sugar
5	tbsp. tamarind juice

PREPARATION:

- Into a blender put the dried chillies, salt, lemon grass, shallots, shrimp paste and a little of the chicken stock and blend well.
- Into a pot pour the remaining chicken stock, add the blended ingredients, and heat to a boil. Next, add sugar, fish sauce and tamarind juice to taste. If not sour enough, add more tamarind juice.
- Then, add the prawns or the fish and the vegetables. Do not overcook.
- Serve hot.
- Serves six.

Tom Yam Kung

(Sour and Spicy Prawn Soup)

INGREDIENTS :

6	large prawns
3	cups chicken stock
5-6	hot chilles, just broken with pestle
2-3	kaffir lime leaves, torn
5	slices galangal
1	lemon grass stem, cut into short sections
2	coriander plants, chopped coarsely
4	tbsp. lime juice
3	tbsp. fish sauce
1/2	lb. mushrooms, halved

PREPARATION:

■ Shell and devein the prawns; then, wash them thoroughly.

■ Heat the stock to boiling. Add the lemon grass, galangal, and prawns; season to taste with lime juice, chillies, and fish sauce. Add kaffir lime leaves, chopped coriander and mushrooms. Remove from the heat, and serve hot.

Instead of chillies, 1 tsp. ground pepper may be mixed with the stock.

■ Serves four.

Tom Yam Kai

(Sour and Spicy Chicken Soup)

INGREDIENTS :

1	lb. boneless chicken meat, diced
3	cups chicken stock
5-6	hot chillies, just broken with pestle
2-3	kaffir lime leaves, torn
6	cherry tomatoes
1	lemon grass stem
4	tbsp. lime juice
3	tbsp. fish sauce
1/2	lb. straw mushrooms, halved
1/2	tsp. sugar

PREPARATION:

■ Cut the lemon grass into 1-inch lengths. Place the stock in a pot, add the lemon grass and kaffir lime leaves, and bring to a boil over medium heat. Add the chicken meat, fish sauce, lime juice and sugar; cook slowly and uncovered for 10 minutes. Do not stir. Then add the tomatoes, mushrooms and chillies and cook for 5 more minutes. Remove from heat.

■ Serves four.

Tom Kha Kai

(Coconut Milk Chicken Soup)

INGREDIENTS :

3 1/2	cups coconut milk
1	lb. chicken (skinned, deboned and diced)
1/2	lb. fresh mushrooms, halved
1	oz. fresh galangal, sliced
1	oz. fresh lemon grass, cut into 1" lengths
4-5	kaffir lime leaves, torn in half
2-3	fresh chillies, halved
1/3	cup lime juice
3	tbsp. fish sauce
3	tsp. sugar
1	tsp. salt
2	tbsp. chopped coriander greens
1	tbsp. roasted chilli sauce (nam phrik phao) **(see page 23)**

PREPARATION:

■ Put coconut milk into a medium-sized pot, add 1 cup water and bring to a boil over medium heat. Reduce heat, add the galangal, lemon grass, kaffir lime leaves and cook for a few more minutes, stirring occasionally. Next, add the chicken, salt, fish sauce, sugar and lime juice, cook until the chicken is done. Then, add the mushrooms and remove from heat.

■ To Serve: Put 1 tbsp. of roasted chilli sauce in the bottom of a large serving bowl. Pour in the boiling soup.

■ Serves four.

Kaeng Liang Ruam Phak

(Fish-Flavored Vegetable Soup)

INGREDIENTS FOR SPICE MIXTURE :

10	pepper corns
1	tbsp. shrimp paste
10	shallots
1/2	cup dried shrimp or fish

OTHER INGREDIENTS :

5	cups (18 oz.) sponge gourd, bottle-gourd, or other gourd, and baby corn
5	stems of sweet basil (maenglak)
4	cups soup stock or water
2-3	tbsp. fish sauce

PREPARATION:

- Place spice mixture ingredients in a mortar and pound until mixed thoroughly.
- Add spice mixture to soup stock (or water) in a pot and heat to boiling, stirring to prevent sticking. Do not cover the pot or allow to boil over.
- Wash the vegetables. If gourd is used, peel and cut into 1 /2 inch strips. Other vegetables are separated into individual leaves.
- When the water boils, add fish sauce, or, if the odor of this is offensive, salt may be substituted. Add the vegetables and boil. When vegetables are done, season to taste with fish sauce or salt, as desired; then, remove from heat.
- Serves four.

Kaeng Joet Wun Sen

(Mungbean Noodle Soup)

INGREDIENTS :

1	cup mungbean noodles, soaked and cut into short lengths
2	oz. ear mushroom or champignon
1	cup chopped or finely sliced pork
5	small prawns
1	tsp. finely sliced coriander root
1/4	tsp. pepper
5	cloves garlic
2	spring onions
3 1/2	cups soup stock
3	tbsp. fish sauce or light soy sauce
2	tbsp. cooking oil

PREPARATION:

■ Pound the coriander root, pepper, and garlic well in a mortar.

■ Heat the oil in a wok. When hot, fry the garlic mixture until fragrant. Add the pork, prawns and some fish sauce, along with 1/2 cup of the stock, the noodles, and the mushrooms.

■ Continue frying for about 5 minutes and then transfer the contents of the wok to a pot, add the remaining soup stock, heat to boiling, and add fish sauce to taste. Remove from the heat, garnish with spring onions and serve.

■ Serves four.

Lap Mu

(Savory Chopped-Pork Salad)

INGREDIENTS :

2	cups ground lean pork
4	oz. pork liver
5-6	tbsp. lime juice
2	tbsp. ground pan-roasted rice or dry breadcrumbs
1/2	tsp. ground chilli
2	tbsp. fish sauce
2	coriander plants, chopped
2	spring onions, sliced
1/2	cup mint leaves
1	tbsp. thinly sliced shallot

PREPARATION:

■ Mix the pork with 4 tbsp. lime juice and work with squeezing movements of the hand; then, squeeze the pork to drive out excess liquid. Now, immerse the pork in boiling water, stir, and remove from the water when done.

■ Boil the liver until done and then cut into small, thin slices.

■ Mix the pork, liver, pan-roasted rice (or breadcrumbs), ground chilli, shallots, spring onions and coriander greens; season to taste with the fish sauce and the remaining lime juice. Sprinkle with mint leaves and serve with lettuce, cabbage, and yard-long beans.

■ Serves four.

Lap Kai

(Savory Chopped-Chicken Salad)

INGREDIENTS :

3	cups coarsely chopped chicken
5	thinly sliced shallots
3	sliced spring onions
1/4	cup lime juice
1	tsp. salt
1/2	tsp. ground chilli
2	tbsp. ground pan-roasted rice or dry breadcrumbs
1/4	cup coarsely chopped coriander greens
1/4	cup mint leaves

PREPARATION:

■ Mix the chicken and the salt, place in a covered baking dish, and bake at 400°F. for about ten minutes or until done. After removing from the oven and allowing to cool somewhat, knead to break up the mass of baked chicken.

■ Add the ground chilli, pan-roasted rice (or breadcrumbs), shallots, spring onions, and lime juice; toss gently. Add the mint leaves and corinader greens, toss once again, arrange upon a bed of lettuce, and serve with sliced cucumber, yard-long beans, and cabbage.

■ Serves four.

Neua Nam Tok

(Savory Beef Salad)

INGREDIENTS :

1	lb. beef cut into thin strips about 1 inch wide and 2 inches long
1	tbsp. thinly sliced lemon grass
1 1/2	tbsp. well-pounded parched rice
1/2	cup thinly sliced shallot
1/2	cup coarsely chopped mint leaves
4 1/2	tbsp. lime juice
3	tbsp. fish sauce
1/2	cup chopped coriander greens
1/2	tsp. ground dried chilli
1	tbsp. chopped spring onion
1/4	tsp. sugar
1	lettuce plant

PREPARATION:

- Grill sliced beef strips to medium rare.
- In a mixing bowl, mix all remaining ingredients well, add beef and toss well.
- Serve the beef on a bed of lettuce with spring onions.
- Serves three to four.

Yam Kai Yang

(Spicy Barbecued-Chicken Salad)

INGREDIENTS FOR SPICE SAUCE DRESSING :

1	tbs. ground chilli
2	tbsp. vinegar
2	tbsp. lime juice
1	tbsp. sugar
2	tbsp. fish sauce
1/2	tsp. salt

OTHER INGREDIENTS :

1	barbecued chicken
1	thinly sliced onion
1	thinly sliced tomato
1 1/2	tbsp. ground roasted peanuts
3-4	lettuce leaves

PREPARATION:

- Make up the dressing by mixing all ingredients and then heating to a boil. Add the peanuts.
- Separate the chicken into pieces and cut each piece diagonally into thin slices.
- Pour the dressing onto the chicken and stir lightly. Add the onion and tomato, stir again.
- Arrange the salad onto a bed of lettuce arranged on a platter, serve with fresh vegetables, such as cabbage.
- Serves four to five.

Yam Pla Meuk

(Spicy Squid Salad)

INGREDIENTS FOR DRESSING :

2	tbsp. sliced garlic
2-3	hot chillies
1/4	cup lime juice
3-4	tbsp. fish sauce

PREPARATION:

- Pound the chillies and garlic well in a mortar and mix with the lime juice and fish sauce.

INGREDIENTS :

1	lb. fresh squid
1	cup thinly sliced onion
1/4	cup thinly sliced young ginger
1	cup celery cut into 1-inch lengths
1	lettuce plant
1	coriander plant, root removed and coarsely chopped or mint leaves
1	red chilli, thinly sliced for use as garnish

PREPARATION:

- Wash the squid, remove the bone, eyes, and the skin. Cut across the squid into about 1 cm.-thick rings or score (i.e., make shallow cuts with the knife on the outer surface of the squid in a criss-cross pattern). Then, cut the squid into 1 1/2 inch pieces.
- Scald the squid in boiling water. Do not leave the squid in the water long, for it will become tough.
- Gently toss the squid together with the onion, ginger, celery, and the dressing, and if necessary, season with additional fish sauce or lime juice.
- Arrange lettuce leaves around the edge of a serving dish, place the squid salad in the middle, and sprinkle with red chilli and coriander or mint leaves.
- Serves four.

Yam Sam Sahai

(Spicy Pork, Prawn, and Chicken Salad)

INGREDIENTS :

1 1/2	cups sliced steamed pork
1 1/2	cups sliced steamed chicken
1 1/2	cups sliced steamed prawns
	(In each case, the slices should be cut on a diagonal to the grain of the meat.)
3	tbsp. roasted chilli sauce(nam phrik phao) **(See page 23)**
3	tbsp. fish sauce
1/4	cup lime juice
1	tsp. sugar
2-3	tbsp. tamarind juice
1/4	cup roasted peanuts or cashew nuts, broken into chunks
1	Chinese radish
1	carrot
1/2	cup chopped celery
1/2	cup mint leaves
2	head romain lettuce
1/2	head cabbage
5	spring onions

PREPARATION:

- Make the sauce by mixing the roasted chilli sauce, fish sauce, sugar, and tamarind juice in a pot and heating to a boil. Allow to boil a few moments; then, remove from the heat, add the lime juice, and stir.
- When the sauce has cooled, add the pork, chicken, prawn, and celery, mix thoroughly, and then add the mint. Scoop onto a bed of lettuce prepared on a serving platter, sprinkle with the peanuts or cashews, and serve with spring onions, cabbage, and thin slices of carrot and Chinese radish.
- Serves four.

Phla Mu Op

(Savory Baked Pork Salad)

INGREDIENTS :

1	lb. pork
5	lemon grass stems. Take only the swollen base of the stem, where it is tinged with purple and slice thin.
10	thinly sliced shallots
7	kaffir lime leaves, sliced into thin strips
3	tbsp. chopped coriander greens
3	tbsp. thinly sliced spring onion
1/2	cup mint leaves
10	hot chillies
15	cloves garlic
1/2	tsp. salt
4	tbsp. lime juice
1	tbsp. whiskey
1	tbsp. ground black pepper

fish sauce
sugar

PREPARATION:

- Pound the chillies and garlic together with the salt well in a mortar and then add the lime juice and enough sugar and fish sauce to give the dressing a pleasing flavor.
- Cut the pork into 1-inch pieces, add a little maggi sauce, whiskey, pepper, and sugar, place in an oven-proof dish, and bake at 450°F. for 10 minutes.
- Place the pork on a serving dish, add the prepared lemon grass, shallots, kaffir lime leaves, coriander greens, and spring onions, pour on the dressing. Toss well, and serve immediately.
- Serves four.

Yam Wun Sen

(Spicy Mungbean Noodle Salad)

INGREDIENTS FOR DRESSING :

1	tbsp. thinly sliced coriander root
1	thinly sliced bulb of pickled garlic
1	thinly sliced chilli
1/3	cup vinegar
1/3	cup sugar
1	tsp. salt

PREPARATION:

■ Pound the coriander root, pickled garlic, and chilli well in a mortar. Place this mixture in a pot, add the vinegar, sugar, and salt, and heat. When the mixture comes to a boil, remove from the heat and allow to cool.

INGREDIENTS FOR SALAD :

2	cups short lengths of scalded mungbean noodles
1/2	cup thin slices of boiled pork
1/2	cup thin slices of boiled pork liver
1/2	cup thin slices of boiled prawn
1/2	cup thinly sliced onion
1	cup 1-inch lengths of celery
1	tomato cut into thin wedges
1	lettuce plant
1/4	cup crisp fried dried shrimp

PREPARATION:

■ Mix the noodles, pork, liver, prawns, onions, and celery. Add the dressing and toss gently; then, add the tomato.

■ Place the salad on a bed of lettuce and sprinkle with the fried dried shrimp.

■ Serves four.

Phla Kung

(Savory Prawn Salad)

INGREDIENTS :

10	oz. prawns
5	hot chillies
2	stems lemon grass
3	shallots
20	mint leaves
1	coriander plant
1	tbsp. shredded kaffir lime leaves
1	tbsp. lime juice
1	tbsp. fish sauce

PREPARATION:

- Wash, shell, and devein the prawns. Immerse for a short time in boiling water; the prawns should be not quite done.
- Slice the chillies, lemon grass, and shallots thin.
- Pick the leaves from the coriander plant. Wash them and the mint leaves and then drain.
- Toss the prawns with the lime juice and fish sauce. Add the lemon grass, chillies, shallots, and kaffir lime leaves and toss to mix. The flavor should be spicy.
- Transfer to a serving dish and garnish with coriander and mint leaves.
- Serves two to three.

Naem Sot

(Piquant Chopped Pork Salad)

INGREDIENTS :

1	cup finely chopped pork
1/2	cup finely sliced boiled pig skin
1	tsp. salt
1	tbsp. sliced garlic
3-4	tbsp. lime juice
1/4	cup finely sliced young ginger root
1/4	cup sliced onions
1/4	cup chopped coriander and spring onions
1/2	cup roasted peanuts
1	head romaine lettuce
1-2	tbsp. fried dried chillies

PREPARATION:

- Mix the salt with the pork; then, dry fry over low heat until done, breaking the meat into small fragments. Remove from heat, allow to cool, add the pig skin and mix thoroughly.
- Gently blend in garlic, salt, lime juice, ginger, and onion and season to taste.
- Spoon the mixture onto a bed of lettuce. Sprinkle with coriander and spring onions. Serve with roasted peanuts, fried dried chillies, lettuce and other vegetables.
- Serves two to three.

Som Tam Malako

(Papaya Salad)

INGREDIENTS :

1 peeled and shredded green papaya (about 4 cups)
6 garlic cloves
1 dried chilli soaked in water
7 pepper corns
1 tbsp. tamarind juice
3 tbsp. fish sauce
3 tbsp. palm sugar
2 tbsp. lime juice
1/4 cup ground dried shrimp
1/4 cup lime cut into small cubes
cabbage, lettuce and leaves of chaphlu and various sliced vegetables

PREPARATION:

- Gently crush the shredded papaya in a mortar with a pestle. Remove and set aside.
- Crush the garlic, dried chilli, and pepper corns in mortar, mixing thoroughly.
- Mix the tamarind juice, fish sauce, and sugar in a pot and heat to a boil. Remove from heat, allow to cool, add lime juice, and mix in the chilli mixture
- Add the crushed papaya, the dried shrimp and the lime cubes and mix thoroughly.
- Serve with lettuce and other sliced vegetables of choice.
- Serves four.

Kung Phat Som Makham Piak

(Stir-Fried Prawns in Tamarind Sauce)

INGREDIENTS :

1	lb. jumbo prawns shelled and deveined
2	tbsp. chicken broth or water
1	tsp. salt
1/3	cup tamarind juice
7	fried, dried red chillies
2	tbsp. chopped onion
1	tbsp. fish sauce
1	tbsp. fried minced garlic
2	tbsp. fried sliced shallot
2	tbsp. palm sugar
1/3	cup chopped spring onion
1	red bell pepper thinly sliced
1/4	cup chopped coriander
2	tbsp. vegetable oil

PREPARATION:

- Put the vegetable oil in a wok over medium heat. Brown the onion; add the palm sugar, chicken broth, salt, tamarind juice, fish sauce and chillies, stirring and turning with a spatula.
- When the liquid begins to boil, add the prawns, garlic, shallots and spring onions, and remove when prawns are done.
- Garnish with coriander and red bell pepper.
- Serves two to three.

Kung Kra Thiam

(Garlic Prawn)

INGREDIENTS :

8-12	jumbo prawns, shelled and deveined
2	tbsp. chopped garlic
1	tsp. pepper
1/2	tbsp. fish sauce
1 1/4	tsp. sugar
1	tbsp. chopped coriander root
4	tbsp. vegetable oil
1/2	cup chopped spring onion
1/4	cup chopped or minced ginger

PREPARATION:

- In a wok or big frying pan, heat the oil over high heat. Fry the garlic, coriander root, pepper, sugar, fish sauce and prawns, stirring constantly. Cook for 2 minutes and then add the remaining ingredients, stir well, and remove from heat.
- Serves three to four.

Kung Yang Sot Makham Piak

(Broiled Lobster in Tamarind Sauce)

INGREDIENTS :

2	1 lb lobsters
2 1/2	tbsp. palm sugar
1 1/2	tbsp. fish sauce
1/2	tsp. salt
1	tbsp. chopped coriander root
1/3	cup thinly sliced shallot
1/3	cup chopped coriander greens
2 1/2	tbsp. tamarind juice
4-5	fried dried small red chillies
1 1/2	tbsp. vegetable oil
1	tbsp. finely chopped garlic
1	tbsp. water

PREPARATION:

- Put the oil in a wok over medium heat. Fry the garlic, shallots and coriander root. When browned, remove from the wok and set aside.
- Return the wok to the heat. In it, mix the palm sugar, tamarind juice, salt, chillies, fish sauce, and water. When the mixture comes to a boil, remove from the heat.
- Broil the lobsters and then arrange on a serving platter. Sprinkle them with the fried garlic and shallots and then pour the sauce over them. Just before serving, sprinkle with chopped coriander.
- Serves two.

Kaeng Ka-ri Kung
(Curried Prawns)

INGREDIENTS :

1 1/2	lb. prawns, shelled and deveined
2 1/2	cups coconut milk
1	tbsp. yellow curry paste (Nam Phrik Kaeng) Ka-ri, see p. 24)
2	fresh chillies, deseeded and sliced
1/2	cup cherry tomatoes
2	tbsp. fish sauce
1 1/2	tbsp. sugar
1	tsp. salt

PREPARATION:

- Put 3/4 cups of coconut milk into a wok or pan, bring to boil over medium heat, stirring constantly, and boil for 5 minutes.
- Add the curry paste, stir well, and simmer for 10 minutes.
- Then, add the fish sauce, sugar, salt and remaining coconut milk and simmer for 10 more minutes, stirring regularly.
- Finally, put in the chillies, tomatoes and prawns, bring to a boil, and remove from heat.
- Serve with cucumber relish. (See p. 37)
- Serves four.

Kaeng Matsaman Neua reu Kai reu Mu

(Beef, Chicken, or Pork Massaman Curry)

INGREDIENTS :

3	tbsp. matsaman curry paste (See p. 23)
1	lb. beef, chicken, or pork
1 1/2	lbs. grated coconut or 3 cups coconut milk
2	tbsp. roasted peanuts
5	peeled small onions (4 oz.)
5	small potatoes (4 oz.) peeled and boiled
3	bay leaves
5	roasted cardamom pods
1	piece of roasted cinnamon, 1 cm. long
3	tbsp. palm sugar
2	tbsp. fish sauce
3	tbsp. tamarind juice
3	tbsp. lemon juice

PREPARATION

- Cut beef, chicken, or pork into 2 inch chunks.
- Add 1 1/2 cups warm water to the coconut and squeeze out 3 cups coconut milk. Skim off 1 cup coconut cream to be used in cooking the curry paste. Place the remaining coconut milk in a pot with the chicken, pork, or beef and simmer until tender. (If beef is used, 2 additional cups of coconut milk will be needed because of the longer cooking time required.)
- Heat the coconut cream in a wok until oil appears on surface; then, add the curry paste and cook until fragrant. Spoon this mixture into the pot containing the meat and add the peanuts. Taste and adjust the flavor so it is sweet, salty, and sour by adding sugar, fish sauce, tamarind juice, and lemon juice. Add bay leaves, cardamom, cinnamon, potatoes, and onions, simmer until tender.
- Serve with pickled ginger or cucumber relish. (See p. 37)
- Serves four.

Kaeng Phet Kai Sai No Mai

(Chicken in Red Curry with Bamboo Shoots)

INGREDIENTS :

1	lb. diced, boneless chicken
1	tbsp. red curry paste (See p. 26)
3/4	cup coconut milk
1/2	cup sweet basil leaves (horapha)
5	kaffir lime leaves, halved
1	fresh red chilli (sliced lengthwise into 8 pieces)
1/2	cup sliced zucchini
2	tbsp. fish sauce
1/4	tsp. salt
1/3	cup water
5	oz. bamboo shoots (sliced lengthwise)
1 1/2	tsp. sugar

PREPARATION:

- In a pot, bring half the coconut milk to a slow boil, stirring constantly. Put in the red curry paste and chicken, stir well, and cook until done (about 5 minutes).
- Add the remaining coconut milk, water, bamboo shoots, sugar and fish sauce, and bring slowly to a boil. Add salt to taste.
- Add the zucchini, kaffir lime leaves, and sliced chilli; remove from heat. Garnish with sweet basil.
- Serves four to five.

Ho Mok Mu reu Kai reu Pla
(Steamed Curried Pork, Chicken, or Fish)

INGREDIENTS FOR SPICE MIXTURE :

5	dried chillies, seeds removed and soaked in water
3	garlic bulbs
2	tbsp. finely sliced galangal
2	tbsp. finely sliced lemon grass
1	tsp. finely sliced kaffir-lime rind
2	tsp. finely sliced coriander root
5	pepper corns
1/2	tsp. salt
1	tsp. shrimp paste
1	tsp. finely sliced krachai (if fish is used)

OTHER INGREDIENTS :

1	lb. pork, chicken, or filleted fish
3	tbsp. fish sauce
1	egg
2	cups coconut milk
1	tsp. rice flour
2	cups sweet basil leaves (horapha)
2	tbsp. finely chopped coriander greens
1	finely sliced red chilli
3	tbsp. shredded kaffir-lime leaf

PREPARATION:

- Pound the spice mixture ingredients well in a mortar.
- Chop the pork but not too finely; if chicken is used, cut it into small pieces; if fish is used, cut the fillets into thin slices.
- Skim 3/4 cup coconut cream from the coconut milk, add rice flour, bring to a boil, remove from the heat, and set aside for topping.
- Stir 1 cup coconut milk with the pounded spice mixture, add the meat or fish, the egg, the fish sauce, and then the remaining coconut milk a little at a time. Add 1/2 cup basil leaves, 1 tbsp. coriander greens, and 2 tsp.. kaffir lime leaf and stir to mix in.
- Place the remaining sweet basil leaves in the bottoms of custard cups, fill each cup with the mixture, and steam for 15 minutes. Remove the cups from the steamer, top each one with some of the boiled coconut cream and a little coriander greens, kaffir lime leaf, and sliced chilli, return to the steamer to steam for one minute, and then remove from the steamer.
- Shredded cabbage may be substituted for sweet basil leaves.
- Serves four.

Kaeng Phet Het

(Red Curry of Mushrooms)

INGREDIENTS :

1/2	cup sweet basil leaves (horapha)
1/2	lb. fresh mushrooms (halved)
1	tbsp. red curry paste (See p. 26)
1/2	tbsp. sugar
3	tbsp. fish sauce
1	tsp. chopped kaffir lime leaf
1	sliced whole medium red or green chilli
1 1/2	cups coconut milk
1/2	cup water (or chicken stock)

PREPARATION:

- Put half of the coconut milk in a wok over medium heat. Add the red curry paste and stir until thoroughly mixed.
- Add the remaining coconut milk, chicken stock, mushrooms, fish sauce, sugar, kaffir lime leaves, chilli and basil.
- Do not overcook mushrooms.
- Serves three to four.

Kaeng Khiao Wan Neua

(Thai Beef Curry)

INGREDIENTS :

3	tbsp. green curry paste (See P. 25)
1	lb. beef
1	lb. grated coconut or 2 1/2 cups coconut milk
4	oz. eggplant (makheua phuang)
2	kaffir lime leaves
1/4	cup sweet basil leaves (horapha)
1 1/2-2	tbsp. fish sauce
1	tbsp. palm sugar
1	tbsp. cooking oil

PREPARATION:

- Cut beef into long, thin slices.
- Add 2 cups warm water to the coconut and squeeze out 1 cup coconut cream and 1 1/2 cups coconut milk.
- Fry the curry paste in oil until fragrant, reduce heat, add the coconut cream a little at a time, stirring until the coconut cream begins to have an oily sheen.
- Add the beef and torn kaffir lime leaves and cook a short time; then, pour the curry into a pot, add the coconut milk and sugar. Add fish sauce to taste, and heat. When boiling, add the eggplant. When the meat is done, add the sweet basil and remove from heat.
- Pork or chicken can be used in place of beef.
- Serves four.

Kai Kolae

(Southern-Thai-Style Braised Chicken)

SPICE MIXTURE INGREDIENTS :

5	dried chillies, seeds removed and soaked in water
1	tsp. salt
1/4	tsp. ground roasted coriander seeds
1/4	tsp. ground roasted cumin seeds
1/4	tsp. ground cinnamon
2	tbsp. thinly sliced shallots
1	tbsp. chopped garlic
1	tsp. chopped fresh turmeric or curry powder
1	tsp. shrimp paste

OTHER INGREDIENTS :

1	young chicken weighing about 3 1/2 lbs.
5	cups coconut milk
4	tbsp. butter
2	tbsp. cooking oil
3	tbsp. fish sauce
2	tbsp. palm sugar
3	tbsp. lime juice

PREPARATION:

- Pound the chillies and salt in a mortar. Add the garlic and shallots and pound well; then, add the turmeric (or curry powder) and pound fine. Add the coriander, cumin, and cinnamon and pound to mix well. Finally, add the shrimp paste and mix in thoroughly.
- Clean the chicken, cut into 10-12 pieces, and fry in the butter and cooking oil. When the chicken is golden brown, transfer it to a pot, add the coconut milk, and place on a medium heat. When the coconut milk comes to a boil, reduce the heat and simmer for 30 minutes.
- Place the butter and oil remaining from the frying of the chicken in a wok on a medium heat, and fry the spice mixture. When fragrant, add to the pot and season with fish sauce, lime juice, and palm sugar.
- When the chicken is tender, arrange on a serving platter, garnish with red chillies, and serve with steamed rice.
- Serves four to five.

Pha-naeng Neua

(Beef Curried in Sweet Peanut Sauce)

INGREDIENTS :

1 lb. beef, cut into thin strips
3 tbsp. pha-naeng curry paste (or red curry paste) (See p. 26)
6 fresh or dry kaffir lime leaves (halved)
1/2 cup sweet basil leaves (horapha)
1 fresh chilli (seeded and cut into strips)
2 cups coconut milk
1/3 cup chicken stock
3 tbsp. palm sugar
2 1/2 tbsp. fish sauce
1/4 tsp. salt
1/2 cup ground roasted peanuts

PREPARATION:

- Put the coconut milk into medium-sized sauce pan over medium heat, add the curry paste and slowly bring to a boil, stirring constantly.
- Put in beef strips and cook for 5 minutes.
- Meanwhile, in a bowl, mix the rest of the ingredients except for the sweet basil and fresh chilli. Add this to the curried beef, and simmer about 15 minutes. Add the sweet basil and fresh chilli, stir well, and remove from the heat.
- Serves four to five.

Pik Kai Sot Sai Pha-naeng

(Stuffed Chicken Wings in Pha-naeng Sauce)

INGREDIENTS

3	tbsp. red curry paste (See p. 26)
12	chicken wings
1	cup chopped chicken breast
4	cups coconut milk
3	tbsp. fish sauce
2	tbsp. palm sugar
2	tbsp. shredded kaffir lime leaf
1/2	cup sweet basil leaves (horapha)
1	tbsp. thinly sliced chilli

PREPARATION:

- Slit open the wings, remove the bones, being careful not to tear the skin, and cut off the pointed tip of each wing (see p. 26).
- Blend the chicken breast with 1 tbsp. of the curry paste and 1 tbsp. fish sauce.
- Put some of the stuffing into each wing but do not pack too tightly.
- Close the slit by pinning the skin on either side together with a sliver of bamboo and shape so they look like chicken wings. Then, place the wings in a steamer and steam until done; 15 minutes.
- Place 1 cup of coconut milk in a wok over medium heat. When some oil has surfaced, add the remaining curry paste and stir to disperse. When fragrant, add the remaining coconut milk a little at a time and season with fish sauce and sugar. Now, add the steamed chicken wings and season as necessary. Transfer the wings and sauce to a pot, close the lid, and simmer over a very low heat until the wings are tender and the liquid is much reduced in volume.
- Place the wings on a serving dish and garnish with the kaffir lime leaf, chilli, sweet basil leaves, and coriander greens.
- Serves four to six.

Kaeng Chuchi Pla

(Fish Curry)

INGREDIENTS :

3	tbsp. red curry paste (See p. 26)
1	lb. mackerel or other meaty fish
3	cups coconut milk
3	tbsp. fish sauce
2	tbsp. palm sugar
2	kaffir lime leaves cut into thin strips

PREPARATION:

- Wash and clean the fish, remove the head, and score diagonally on both sides.
- Deep fry the fish in hot oil until golden brown. Remove from oil and drain. Set aside.
- Heat 1 cup coconut milk in a wok until some of the oil surfaces, add the curry paste and cook, stirring until dispersed and fragrant; then, add the rest of the coconut milk, when it comes to a boil, add the fish. Cook for two minutes moving the fish around gently.
- Season to taste with fish sauce and palm sugar. Remove from heat.
- Arrange on a serving plate and garnish with shreds of kaffir lime leaf.

Kaeng Phet Pet Yang

(Red Curry of Duck)

INGREDIENTS :

1	roasted duck, deboned and cut into 1″ squares
2 1/2	cups coconut milk
1 1/2	tbsp. vegetable oil
3	tbsp. red curry paste (See p. 26)
2	medium tomatoes, halved or 10 cherry tomatoes
1/2	cup sweet basil leaves (horapha)
4	kaffir lime leaves, halved
1/2	tsp. salt
2	tbsp. fish sauce
1	tsp. sugar
1/2	cup water (or chicken stock)

PREPARATION:

- Put vegetable oil into wok over medium heat and add the red curry paste, stir well, add 3/4 cups coconut milk and stir to mix thoroughly.
- Add the duck and stir well. Next, add the remaining coconut milk, water, tomatoes, kaffir lime leaves, sugar, salt, fish sauce and sweet basil.
- Cook for about 10 minutes or until duck absorbs curry flavor.
- Serves six.

Kaeng Khua Fak Kap Kai

(Chicken and Wax Gourd Curry)

INGREDIENTS :

3	tbsp. kaeng khua curry paste (See p. 24)
1	lb. chicken
1	lb. grated coconut or 3 cups coconut milk
1	lb. wax gourd
1	tbsp. tamarind juice
3	tbsp. palm sugar
3	tbsp. fish sauce

PREPARATION:

- Clean the chicken, cut into 1 inch pieces.
- Peel the gourd, remove the seeds, and cut it into 1 inch chunks.
- Add 1 1/2 cups warm water to the coconut and squeeze out 3 cups coconut milk.
- Skim off 1 cup coconut cream, place in a wok and heat. When oil begins to appear on the surface, add the spice mixture and stir in, then add the chicken and cook. Spoon into a pot, add the remaining coconut milk and the wax gourd and heat. When the gourd is done, season to taste with tamarind juice, palm sugar, and fish sauce.
- Serves four.

Thai White Wine
THE UNITED PRODUCTS CO.,LTD

Pla Kao Rat Sot Ma-kheua Thet

(Rock Cod Baked in Banana Leaf)

INGREDIENTS :

1	whole banana leaf (or foil)
1	medium-sized whole rock cod
1	cup tender Chinese kale
1/2	cup chopped canned pineapple
1	onion, sliced
1	large tomato, sliced
2	bell peppers, sliced
1/2	cup tomato sauce
1 1/2	tbsp. fish sauce
1	tbsp. dry white wine
1	tsp. sugar
1	tsp. pepper
1	tbsp. butter

PREPARATION:

- Lightly butter an 8 by 10 inch piece of banana leaf (or foil). Put cleaned and scaled fish onto the center of the leaf. Pour tomato sauce and wine, along with the fish sauce and all remaining ingredients, over the fish. Wrap the fish, sealing it in the leaf, tie if necessary, and bake in an oven heated to 350°F. for 15-20 minutes.
- Serves two to three.

Pla Kaphong Khao Neung Phrik Sot Manao

(Sea Perch Steamed with Chillies in Lime Sauce)

INGREDIENTS :

1	sea perch weighing about 18 oz.
6	peeled cloves of giant garlic
5	hot chillies
3	tbsp. lime juice
2	spring onions
1	cup chicken stock
1 1/2	tbsp. light soy sauce

PREPARATION:

- Scale, clean, and wash the fish. With a knife, score the flesh along the length of the fish; then, place it in a deep bowl.
- Chop the chillies and mix them with the chicken stock, lime juice, and soy sauce. The dominant taste should be sour.
- Pour the mixture over the fish and place the spring onions cut into 1 inch lengths and the garlic alongside.
- After the water has begun boiling, place the fish in a steamer and steam over high heat for about 15 minutes. Remove from the steamer and serve hot.
- Serves two to three.

Kung Phao

(Charcoal-Broiled Lobster with Savory Sauce)

INGREDIENTS :

4	medium-sized lobsters
1 1/2	tbsp. chopped garlic
1	tbsp. sugar
1/2	tsp. salt
1/3	cup hot water
1/2	tbsp. chopped chillies
1	tsp. chopped fresh coriander
2	tbsp. lime juice

banana leaf (or foil)

PREPARATION:

- Clean the lobsters, wrap each in banana leaf, and tie well. Grill over a charcoal fire about 12 minutes. Serve with the sauce.
- Heat the sugar and water in a sauce pan over low heat, stirring until the sugar is dissolved. Turn off the heat, add the salt and stir well. Remove from heat and allow to cool; then, add the rest of the ingredients and mix thoroughly.
- Serves four.

Khai Tun

(Beaten Egg Steamed with Pork)

INGREDIENTS :

2	eggs
3	tbsp. ground pork
2	tbsp. thinly sliced shallot
1/4	tsp. pepper
2	tbsp. light soy sauce
1	cup chicken stock
1	tbsp. chopped spring onion
1/4	tsp. salt
3	prawns, shelled and deveined

PREPARATION:

- Beat the eggs in a mixing bowl, add the shallots, the stock, the pepper, light soy sauce and salt, stirring with a fork.
- Divide the mixture into 3 portions. Put each portion into a small glass bowl.
- Wrap each prawn with 1/3 of the pork.
- After the water has begun boiling, place the cups in a steamer and steam until the egg mixture begins to cook. Place a prawn on top of the mixture in each cup. Continue steaming until the pork and prawns are done; about 10-15 minutes.
- Remove the cups from the steamer and sprinkle with chopped spring onion. Serve hot.
- Serves three.

Pu Ja
(Stuffed Crab)

INGREDIENTS :

3 meaty crabs
1 cup ground pork
2 eggs
1/2 tbsp. minced coriander root
1 tsp. minced garlic
1/4 tsp. pepper
1 tbsp. light soy sauce
1/2 tsp. salt
3 tbsp. fine breadcrumbs
2 cups cooking oil
coriander leaves and red spur chilli

PREPARATION:

■ Wash the crabs and then steam them whole. When done, remove all the meat, saving the shells for stuffing.

■ Knead together the crabmeat, pork, coriander root, garlic, pepper, soy sauce, salt, and one egg. When well mixed, pack this filling into crab shells.

■ Pour the oil into a frying pan and place on medium heat.

■ Beat the remaining egg well, add the beaten egg onto the exposed surface of the filling, and then sprinkle with breadcrumbs.

■ When the oil is hot, put the crabs into it with the exposed surface of the filling downward. When the surface of the filling turns golden brown, lift the crabs from the oil, drain, garnish with coriander leaves and chilli shreds, and serve with chilli sauce.

■ If crabmeat is bought ready steamed and without shells, pack the filling into small over-proof cups and add the beaten egg onto the exposed surface of the filling, and then sprinkle with breadcrumb. Bake at 350° F for 15 minutes or until golden brown. Then remove from the oven and allow to cool down before taking the filling out of the cups to serve.

■ Serves four.

Pla Meuk Yat Sai

(Sautéed Stuffed Squid)

INGREDIENTS :

6-8 medium-sized fresh whole squid
1/2 lb. ground pork
1 tsp. chopped coriander
1/4 tsp. pepper
1 tbsp. chopped garlic
1 tsp. fish sauce
1 tsp. sugar
1 tbsp. light soy sauce
1 egg (slightly beaten)
1 tsp. chopped onion

PREPARATIONS:

■ Clean the squid and set aside. In a bowl, mix the rest of the above ingredients by hand. Stuff this filling into the whole squid and steam for 15 minutes. Then, cut diagonally into slices.

■ Into the 1/4 cup of hot vegetable oil, add the sliced stuffed squid along with the remaining ingredients listed below and fry for 5 minutes. Drain and serve with steamed rice.

2 tsp. sliced fresh ginger
1/2 cup spring onion cut in 1" lengths
1/2 cup sliced Shiitake mushroom
1 tbsp. oyster sauce
1/4 cup oil
1 tsp. minced garlic

■ Serves six.

Pla Jalamet Khao Thot

(Fried White Pompano)

INGREDIENTS :

1	white pompano weighing about 1 lb.
1	tbsp. tapioca flour
3-4	thinly sliced hot chillies
1-2	thinly sliced shallots
1	tsp. lime juice
2	tbsp. fish sauce
3	cups cooking oil

PREPARATION:

■ Clean and wash the fish. With a knife, score both sides of the fish attractively. Then, turn the fish in the flour to coat on all sides.

■ Place the oil in a frying pan on medium heat. When the oil is hot, fry the fish until golden brown. Remove the fish from the pan and drain.

■ Serve with a sauce made by mixing the shallots, chilli, fish sauce, and lime juice.

■ Serves two.

Pla Jalamet Khao Neung Kiam Buai

(Steamed White Pompano with Pickled Plum)

INGREDIENTS :

1	white pompano weighing about 1 lb.
2	pickled plums
1/2	cup long, thin strips of pork fat
2	celery plants (see page 20)
1/2	cup rice-straw mushrooms
1	tsp. light soy sauce
1	tsp. shredded ginger
1	red chilli, sliced lengthwise into thin strips

PREPARATION:

- Clean and wash the fish. With a knife, make several cuts on each side in a criss-cross design. Place the fish on a platter for steaming.
- Mix the pork fat strips with the pickled plums and soy sauce and then pour over the fish.
- Slice the mushrooms and the celery into short lengths. Place these and the chilli and ginger on the fish.
- Place the platter containing the fish in a steamer in which the water is already boiling. Steam at high heat for about 15 minutes.
- Serves two.

Si-Khrong Mu Phat Priao Wan

(Sweet and Sour Spareribs)

INGREDIENTS :

2	lbs. spareribs, cut into 1 1/2 inch lengths and marinated 2-3 hours in 1 tbsp. light soy sauce, 1 tsp. ground pepper, 1 tsp. salt, 1 tsp. corn flour, and 1 tsp. Chinese wine
1/4	cup chilli, sliced diagonally
1/2	cup pineapple, sliced into cubes
1/2	cup onion rings
1/4	cup tomato, cut in quarters

INGREDIENTS FOR THE SWEET AND SOUR SAUCE :

1/2	cup tomato catsup
1/4	cup shredded fresh young ginger
1	tbsp. vinegar
1	tbsp. sugar
1	tsp. salt
1/2	tsp. pepper
3	cups soup stock

PREPARATION:

- Fry the marinated spareribs until golden brown in 1/2 cup cooking oil; then, remove from the pan and drain.
- Mix the ingredients for the sweet and sour sauce in a pot, heat to boiling, then simmer about 15 minutes. Strain the sauce to remove any lumps. When ready to serve:
- Place the fried pork ribs on a platter.
- Heat 1/4 cup oil in a wok until very hot. Put the chillies, pineapple, tomatoes, and onions into the wok and fry. Add 1 cup of the sweet and sour sauce. In a bowl, mix 2 tbsp. corn starch with 3 tbsp. cold water, and add, as much of this as required to the mixture in the pan to thicken it; then, spoon it over the spareribs.
- Serves four to five.

Phat Mu Priao Wan

(Sweet and Sour Pork)

INGREDIENTS :

1 lb. lean pork, sliced into thin 2″ × 1″ strips
3 oz. straw mushrooms, sliced
1 large tomato, sliced
1 cup 1-inch lengths of spring onion
1 tsp. chopped garlic
2 fresh chillies, deseeded and sliced
1/2 cup chicken stock
1 tbsp. vinegar
2 tbsp. tomato sauce
2 tbsp. sugar
1 tbsp. vegetable oil
1 tbsp. fish sauce
1 tbsp. tapioca flour
1/4 tbsp. pepper
1/3 cup sliced onion
1/4 tsp. salt
1 tbsp. chopped coriander greens
1/2 cup sliced cucumber

PREPARATION:

- Heat the oil in a wok over medium-high heat and brown the garlic. Add the pork and cook for 5 minutes, stirring constantly. Then, add the mushrooms, tomato, spring onions, chillies, vinegar, tomato sauce, sugar, fish sauce, onions, salt and half of the chicken stock. Stir well.
- Mix the remaining chicken stock with the tapioca flour, blend well and pour slowly into the wok and cook until the sauce thickens. Season with pepper and remove from heat. Garnish with coriander and cucumber.
- Serves four.

Kung Op Wun Sen

(Baked Prawns and Mungbean Noodles)

INGREDIENTS :

1	lb. prawns
5	coriander roots, crushed
1	tbsp. pepper corns
1	onion, thinly sliced
3	slices ginger, crushed
2	tbsp. cooking oil
1	tbsp. Maggi sauce
1/4	tsp. salt
1	tbsp. sugar
1	tbsp. oyster sauce
2	tbsp. light soy sauce
1	tsp. sesame oil
1	tbsp. whiskey
2	cups mungbean noodles, soaked and cut into short lengths

PREPARATION:

- Place the oil in a wok, heat, and stir fry the coriander root, ginger, pepper, and onion. When fragrant, remove from the wok and place in a mixing bowl.
- Add the noodles, the sauces, salt, sugar, seasame oil and whiskey, toss the noodles until well coated, and then add the prawns and toss well once again.
- Divide the noodles and prawns into four individual portions; place each portion in a lidded cup, and close the lids. Place the cups on a baking tray and bake at 450° F. until the prawns are done (about 10 minutes).
- Serve hot with fresh vegetables, such as tomatoes and spring onions.
- Serves four.

Kung Neung Si Iu

(Prawns Steamed with Soy Sauce)

INGREDIENTS :

12	prawns
2	tsp. light soy sauce
2	coriander roots, chopped
1	tsp. oyster sauce
1	tbsp. chopped garlic
1	tbsp. finely chopped spring onion
1/4	tsp. pepper

PREPARATION:

- Shell and devein the prawns and arrange on a plate.
- Mix the garlic and coriander root with the soy sauce and the oyster sauce; then, pour over the prawns.
- After the water has already begun to boil, place the prawns in the steamer. Steam about 10 minutes, remove, sprinkle with the spring onion and pepper, and serve.
- Serves four.

Pla Samli Daet Diao

(Fried Sun-Dried Kingfish)

INGREDIENTS :

1	kingfish weighing 1 lb.-1 1/2 lbs.
1	tbsp. finely sliced shallot
2	tbsp. shredded green mango
1	tsp. shredded hot chilli
2	tbsp. fish sauce
3	tbsp. lime juice
1	tsp. palm sugar
2	cups cooking oil

PREPARATION:

- Wash, clean and butterfly the fish leaving the two sides joined along the belly. Open the fish out flat so that the skin is downward, remove the bones, and score the flesh with a knife.
- After allowing it to dry, lay the fish opened out flat in strong sunshine for five to six houres, turning regularly so the sun strikes both the skin side and the interior.
- Pour the oil into a deep frying pan and place on a medium heat. When the oil is hot, place the fish, still opened out, in the oil. When the lower side becomes crisp and golden, turn the fish and continue frying until it is done on both sides; then, remove from the pan, drain, place on a serving dish.
- Toss the shallots, mango, and chilli together, seasoning with fish sauce, lime juice, and palm sugar so that a sour taste is the predominant one. Spoon into a bowl and serve with the fish.
- Serves two to three.

Pla Pae-Sa
(Steamed Fish)

INGREDIENTS :

1	fish weighing about 1 lb. (suitable are such meaty fish as serpent head)
1/4	cup shredded ginger
1/4	cup thin slices of pork fat
2	pickled garlic bulbs sliced thin
1	celery plant chopped into short lengths (see page 20)
1	red chilli sliced diagonally
2	cups chicken stock
3	tbsp. vinegar
2	tsp. sugar

PREPARATION:

- Clean and scale the fish. Score it on both sides. Place it in a deep dish, lay the strips of pork fat upon it, and steam in a steamer on high heat for 10 minutes.
- Remove the fish from the steamer and arrange upon it first, the celery, the pickled garlic, and then the chilli.
- Mix the chicken stock, vinegar and sugar, stir until the sugar has dissolved, and then pour into the dish containing the fish. Return the dish to the steamer and steam over vigorously boiling water for about ten minutes; then, remove from the steamer and serve with the sauce.

INGREDIENTS FOR SAUCE :

5	hot chillies
1	tbsp. chopped crushed garlic
1	tbsp. sugar
2	tbsp. lime juice
1	tsp. finely ground roasted peanuts
1	tsp. salt

PREPARATION:

- Pound the chillies, garlic, sugar, and salt together in a mortar, mix in the peanuts and lime juice, transfer to a small bowl.
- Serves two.

Kai Phat Kap Haeo

(Stir Fried Chicken with Water Chestnuts)

INGREDIENTS :

1	lb. chicken
1/4	cup cooking oil
1	garlic plant
4	slices fresh ginger
1/4	cup light soy sauce
1	tbsp. sherry
1	cup water
10	canned water chestnuts
1/2	tbsp. sugar
1	tbsp. coarsely chopped celery

PREPARATION:

- Wash the garlic plant and cut into two-inch sections. Wash the chicken and cut into bite-sized chunks.
- Heat the oil in a wok. When hot, put in the ginger and garlic plant together with the chicken, stir-fry until chicken is golden brown. Add the soy sauce, the sherry and the water; then, cover the wok and reduce to low heat.
- Add the water chestnuts and then the sugar; cook over low heat for 15 minutes until the chicken is tender. Then, spoon onto a serving platter, sprinkle with the celery, and serve hot.
- Serves four.

Phat Khi Mao Kai reu Mu

(Spicy Stir-Fried Chicken or Pork)

INGREDIENTS :

5	hot chillies
4	coriander roots
2	tbsp. fish sauce
1	tbsp. oyster sauce
2	tbsp. cooking oil
5	cloves garlic
1/2	cup whole basil leaves (ka-prao)
1	tsp. sugar
2	cups ground chicken or pork

chicken stock

PREPARATION:

- Pound the garlic, chilies, and coriander roots well in a mortar.
- Heat the oil in a wok. When the oil is hot, add the pounded chilli mixture and stir-fry. When the garlic is golden brown, add the meat and continue stirring and turning.
- When the meat is done, add the oyster sauce, fish sauce, sugar, and enough chicken stock to give the dish some liquid. Add the basil leaves and stir. Serve with rice.
- Serves four.

Phat Phet Mu

(Stir-Fried Pork with Red Curry Paste)

INGREDIENTS :

1	lb. lean pork sliced into thin strips about 1 inch wide and 2 inches long
1	tbsp. red curry paste (See p. 26)
3	kaffir lime leaves torn in half
1	tbsp. green pepper corns
1	cup coconut milk
1/2	cup sweet basil leaves (horapha)
3/4	cup sliced baby zucchini
1 1/2	tbsp. fish sauce
1/4	tsp. salt
1	tbsp. sugar
1	tbsp. vegetable oil
2	fresh red chillies, deseeded and sliced

PREPARATION:

- ■ Heat oil in wok over medium heat. Fry the red curry paste and pork for 5 minutes, stirring regularly. Add half of the coconut milk and cook for another 10 minutes, stirring occasionally.
- ■ When the pork is done, add the remaining coconut milk, the fish sauce, kaffir lime leaves, salt and sugar, stir well and bring to a boil.
- ■ Then, add the zucchini, pepper corns and chillies, and stir well.
- ■ Garnish with basil.
- ■ Serves four.

Phat Phrik Khing Mu Kap Thua Fak Yao

(Savory Stir-Fried Pork with Yard-long Beans)

INGREDIENTS FOR CURRY PASTE :

3	dried chillies
7	shallots
2	garlic bulbs
1	tsp. galangal
1	tbsp. chopped lemon grass
5	pepper corns
1	tsp. chopped coriander root
1	tsp. grated kaffir lime rind
1	tsp. salt
1	tsp. shrimp paste
2	tbsp. ground dried shirmp

OTHER INGREDIENTS :

1	lb. pork
1/2	lb. yard-long beans
2	tbsp. cooking oil
1	tbsp. palm sugar
2	tbsp. fish sauce

PREPARATION:

- Place the chilli paste ingredients in a mortar and pound until thoroughly ground and mixed.
- Wash the pork, cut into long, thin slices, and marinate in 1 tbsp. fish sauce.
- Wash the beans, cut into 1 inch lengths, boil until just cooked, and remove from the water.
- Heat the oil in a wok, fry the pork until done, then remove the pork from the pan and set aside.
- Put the chilli paste in the wok and fry until fragrant, then add the pork, sugar, fish sauce, and yard-long beans. Stir-fry until thoroughly mixed, remove from heat and serve.
- Serves four.

Phat Phrik Khing Kai

(Savory Stir-Fried Chicken)

INGREDIENTS :

phrik khing curry paste (see the facing page)

1/2	cup coconut milk
1 1/2	lbs. sliced chicken breast
1/4	lb. bacon, fried crisp
4	kaffir lime leaves, torn into quarters
3	tbsp. vegetable oil
2	tbsp. fish sauce
1	tbsp.sugar

PREPARATION:

- Put oil into a wok over medium heat. Add the phrik khing curry paste and stir well. Next add the coconut milk and chicken, stirring regularly until the chicken is done. Then add the kaffir lime leaves, fish sauce and sugar to taste. Remove from the heat and sprinkle with bacon.
- Serves four.

Kha Mu Tom Phalo

(Boiled Fresh Ham with the Five Spices)

INGREDIENTS :

1 1/2	lbs. fresh ham
10	cloves garlic
3	coriander roots
1/2	tsp. five spice powder
20	pepper corns
1	tsp. dark soy sauce
2	tbsp. chilli sauce
2	tbsp. light soy sauce

PREPARATION:

■ Place all the ingredients in a pressure cooker and add enough water to nearly cover the ham (about 2 cups). Cover and cook about 20 minutes over medium heat. After removing the pressure cooker from the heat, allow it to cool (at least 10 minutes) before opening. Remove the bone from the ham, place the meat and the liquid in a serving dish and sprinkle with chopped coriander greens. Serve with the sauce.

INGREDIENTS FOR SAUCE :

2	yellow chillies
1	coriander root
10	cloves garlic
1/2	tsp. salt
2	tbsp. vinegar

PREPARATION:

■ Place the chillies, coriander root, garlic, and salt in a mortar and break up with the pestle. Mix in the vinegar and transfer to a small bowl.

■ Serves four to six.

Mu Tom Khem
(Stewed Pork)

INGREDIENTS :

2	lbs. tenderloin of pork (cut into cubes)
1	tsp. salt
1	tbsp. pepper corns
1	tbsp. chopped garlic
1	tbsp. chopped fresh coriander root
1	tbsp. brandy
3	tbsp. fish sauce
1	tbsp. vegetable oil
1/4	cup dark soy sauce
1 1/2	tbsp. palm sugar
2	cups water (or chicken broth)
4	shelled hard-boiled eggs

PREPARATION:

■ Into a blender put the pepper corns, coriander root, garlic, dark soy sauce, fish sauce, salt, palm sugar, brandy, and 1 cup of water, and blend well. Marinate the pork in this mixture for 20 minutes.

■ Heat oil in a wok over high heat and stir fry the pork with the marinade. Then, add 1 cup of water and the eggs, lower the heat, and simmer for 20 minutes.

■ Serves four to six.

Phat Neua Namman Hoi

(Stir-Fried Beef in Oyster Sauce)

INGREDIENTS :

1	lb. thin slices of tender beef
1	tbsp. wheat flour
3	tbsp. cooking oil
1	tsp. sugar
1/2	tsp. pepper
5	oz. straw mushrooms or champignons
2	tbsp. light soy sauce
4	tbsp. oyster sauce
1	spring onion cut into short lengths
1	tbsp. finely chopped garlic

PREPARATIONS:

- Marinate the beef slices in a mixture of the flour and light soy sauce.
- Place the oil in a wok over medium heat. Fry the garlic until fragrant and then add the mushrooms. When the mushrooms are tender, put in the beef and continue stir-frying until it is done.
- Add the oyster sauce, sugar, and pepper, stir to mix well, add the spring onion, stir well and serve.
- Serves three to four.

Phat Kha-na Namman Hoi

(Stir-Fried Kai Lan in Oyster Sauce)

INGREDIENTS:

10	kai lan plants of equal size
20	champignons or rice-straw mushrooms
3	tbsp. cooking oil
1	tbsp. finely chopped garlic
4	tbsb. oyster sauce
1	tsp. salt
1/4	tsp. pepper
1	tsp. sugar
1/4	cup chicken stock

PREPARATION:

- Wash the kai lan well, remove the old leaves, the old part of the stem, and the tough outer covering of the stem.
- Wash the mushrooms and remove any inedible portions.
- To boiling water, add 1 tsp. salt. Parboil kai lan, remove from hot water immediately and submerge in cold water. Scald the mushrooms in a similar manner. Drain both the kai lan and the mushrooms.
- Heat the oil in a wok. When it is hot, fry the garlic. When it is fragrant, add the kai lan and the mushrooms, stir to mix well, and then add the chicken stock, oyster sauce, sugar, and pepper. Stir well, remove from heat and serve.
- Serves four.

Phat Ma-kheua Yao

(Stir-Fried Chicken with Long Eggplant)

INGREDIENTS :

1/2	lb. chicken breast, deboned and sliced
1	cup sliced long eggplant
1/3	cup sweet basil leaves (horapha)
2	fresh chillies, deseeded and sliced
1/2	tbsp. chopped garlic
1/2	tbsp. soybean paste
1	tbsp. fish sauce
1	tbsp. dark soy sauce
2	vegetable oil
3	tbsp. water (or chicken stock)

PREPARATION:

- Heat oil in a wok over medium heat. Fry the garlic. When it yellows put in the chicken and cook for 5 minutes. Then, add eggplant and cook for another 5 minutes. Stir in the soybean paste, fish sauce, and dark soy sauce, and cook for 2 minutes. Add the water (or chicken stock), chillies, and basil and slowly bring to a boil. Remove from heat and serve.
- Serves four.

Phat Phak Anamai

(Stir-Fried Prawns with Vegetables)

INGREDIENTS :

1	young sponge gourd
10	ears baby corn
10	rice-straw mushrooms or champignons
12	prawns
1	tbsp. chopped garlic
3	tbsp. cooking oil
1/2	tsp. salt
3	tbsp. oyster sauce

PREPARATION:

- Peel and wash the sponge gourd and cut into bite-sized pieces. Slice the baby corn and rice-straw mushrooms in half. If champignons are used, scald them before slicing. Shell and devein the prawns.
- Heat the oil in a wok. When it is hot, put in the garlic. When the garlic is fragrant, add the prawns and salt. When the prawns are done, add the baby corn and then the mushrooms. When the mushrooms are done, add the sponge gourd and fry until cooked. Add the oyster sauce and stir thoroughly. Serve hot.
- Serves four.

Phat Himalai

(Stir-Fried Chicken with Cashew Nut)

INGREDIENTS :

1	lb. sliced chicken breast
1/2	cup freshly roasted cashew nuts
1/4	cup fried dried chillies
1/3	cup chopped spring onion
1/2	tbsp. chopped garlic
1 1/2	tbsp. fish sauce
1	tbsp. dark soy sauce
1/4	tsp. salt
2	tbsp. vegetable oil
1	small onion, sliced

PREPARATION:

- Heat oil in wok over medium heat. Fry the garlic. When it has yellowed, add the chicken and cook for 5 minutes, turning regularly. Then, add the roasted cashew nuts, chilies, onion, spring onions, fish sauce, dark soy sauce, and salt and cook 1 minute. Garnish with the chopped spring onions.
- Serves four.

Phat Thua Ngok Kap Mu Krop

(Stir-Fried Bean Sprouts and Crisp-Fried Roasted Pork Belly)

INGREDIENTS :

1	lb. bean sprouts
1/2	lb. crisp-fried roasted pork belly
2	tbsp. light soy sauce
3	tbsp. cooking oil
1	tsp. chopped garlic

PREPARATION:

- Wash the bean sprouts well and then drain in a colander.
- Slice the pork into bite-sized pieces.
- Heat the oil in a wok. When the oil is hot, fry the garlic until golden brown; then, add the pork and the bean sprouts, mix, add the soy sauce, stir, and remove from the heat. Avoid over cooking. Serve hot.

INGREDIENTS FOR CRISP-FRIED ROASTED PORK BELLY :

1	tsp. salt
1	tbsp. maggi sauce
2	cups cooking oil
1	lb. pork belly

PREPARATION:

- Cut the pork belly into half-inch thick strips and marinate in a mixture of the salt and maggi sauce for two hours.
- Place the strips one next to another in a roasting pan and roast in a 350 °F. oven for 30 minutes.
- Heat the oil in a deep wok. Deep fry the pork strips until the skin is golden brown; then, remove from the oil and drain.
- Serves four.

Pet Thot Sot Sai

(Baked Stuffed Duck)

INGREDIENTS :

1	deboned duck with innards
2 1/2	cups chopped pork
1	egg
2	tbsp. pounded mixture of garlic, coriander root and pepper
1/4	cup diced onion
1/4	cup diced carrot
1/4	cup peas
3	tbsp. light soy sauce
2	tbsp. Maggi sauce
2	tbsp. butter
1	tbsp. sugar

INGREDIENTS FOR GRAVY :

1/4	cup juices from the pan in which the duck was baked
1	tbsp. wheat flour
1/4	tsp. salt
1/8	tsp. pepper

PREPARATION:

- Wash the duck and remove the innards. Dice the liver, gizzard, heart, and whatever other organs you like. Using a sharp knife with a small, pointed blade debone the duck. Try to keep as much meat as possible and avoid puncturing the meat with the knife. Start near the vent and work up one side toward the neck. Remove the neck and continue around the neck across the back of the duck. Then, follow the same procedure on the other side. Lift the skeleton free of the flesh and then remove the bones from the legs. When done, turn the duck right side out (see p. 22).
- Mix the pork, pounded garlic mixture, diced innards, peas, carrots, and onion together well, add the egg and mix, season with light soy sauce and maggi sauce. Fill the cavities of the duck with the mixture, sew the duck closed, and tie securely with the thread around the outside into a long, cigar-shaped configuration.
- Place the duck in a baking pan and bake at 350°F. for 40 minutes. Remove the duck from the oven, spread the butter over the outside, and bake at 400° F. for 20 minutes. When the back of the duck has turned dark brown, remove from the oven, allow to cool, and cut into 1/2-inch slices.
- Place the slices on a bed of lettuce on a serving platter, surround with slices of pineapple, tomato, and cucumber, and spoon gravy over the duck.

PREPARATION:

- Heat the duck juices in a wok over low heat. Add the flour, salt, and pepper and stir until the gravy is smooth.
- Serves six to eight.

Ped Yang

(Crispy Duck)

INGREDIENTS :

1	duck weighing about 4 lbs.
2	tsp. minced mature ginger
1	tsp. ground cinnamon
1/2	tsp. nutmeg
1	tsp. pepper
2	tbsp. light soy sauce

PREPARATION:

■ Wash the duck, remove the neck, feet, and innards, and pat dry.

■ Mix the ginger, cinnamon, nutmeg, and pepper. Take 1 tsp. of this mixture and spread it over the inside of the duck; then, sew the duck securely closed. Spread the remainder of the spice mixture over the outside of the duck.

■ Wrap the duck in aluminum foil, place it in a deep roasting pan, bake at 450° F. for one hour. After taking the duck from the overn, allow it to cool about fifteen minutes before removing the aluminum foil.

■ Place the duck on a roasting rack and put it on a cookie sheet. With a fork, puncture the skin of the duck at many places over the entire surface in order to prevent the skin's cracking.

■ Bake the duck at 375°F. for about 30 minutes. Remove the duck from the oven and brush the skin with the light soy sauce. Now, bake at 500 °F. for about 5 minutes, until the skin is crisp and brown. Do not allow it to burn.

■ Serve the duck either split in half or deboned. Alternatively, the skin may be served without the meat. Serve with spring onions, cucumbers, lettuce, celery and dark soy sauce.

■ Serves six.

Mu Yang
(Barbecued Pork)

INGREDIENTS :

2	lb. pork shoulder cut into 2 × 4 × 4 inch pieces
2	tbsp. light soy sauce
2	tbsp. sherry
1	tbsp. sesame oil
4	tbsp. sugar
1	tsp. salt
2	garlic plants cut into 1 inch lengths
2	tsp. juice from freshly pounded ginger
2	tbsp. honey

PREPARATION:

- Marinate pork in the other ingredients about six hours before barbecuing.
- While barbecuing, brush pork with marinade. When done, cut pork into small pieces and arrange on a platter. Serve with sweet chilli sauce (see following recipe) and fresh vegetables such as spring onion, slices of cucumber and tomato.
- Serves four to five.

Kai Yang

(Thai-Style Barbecued Chicken)

INGREDIENTS :

2	lbs. chicken pieces
2	tbsp. chopped fresh ginger
2	tbsp. chopped lemon grass
2	tbsp. chopped coriander root
2	cups light soy sauce
1	tsp. sugar
2	tbsp. pepper
1 1/2	tbsp. curry powder

PREPARATION:

- Mix all the ingredients, except the chicken, in a blender and marinate the chicken in the mixture for at least 6 hours in a refrigerator.
- Broil the chicken slowly over a low fire and serve with sweet chilli sauce.

INGREDIENTS FOR SWEET CHILLI SAUCE :

1	tbsp. ground red chilli
1/2	cup vinegar
1	tsp. salt
1	tbsp. sugar
1	tsp. chopped garlic

PREPARATION:

- Mix all the ingredients in a small pot, put over a medium heat and bring to a boil, stirring. Heat until thickened to a syrupy consistency then remove from heat.
- Serves four to five.

Neua Daet Diao

(Fried Sun-Dried Beef)

INGREDIENTS :

1	lb. beef	1	tbsp. fish sauce
1	garlic bulb	3	coriander roots
1	tsp. curry powder	1	tbsp. sugar
1/2	tsp. pepper	2	tbsp. whiskey
1	tbsp. oyster sauce	3	tbsp. chilli sauce

PREPARATION:

■ After washing the beef, cut it into slices about 1/3 inch thick.

■ Pound the garlic, coriander root, and pepper in a mortar. Add the beef slices and work them around in the mixture. Add the fish sauce, oyster sauce, whiskey, sugar, and curry powder, mix well, and allow to marinate for one hour.

■ Arrange the slices of beef on a rack and leave in the sun for one day. Turn occasionally.

■ Fry the sun-dried beef in hot oil and then drain. Serve with sweet chilli sauce (see previous recipe).

■ Serves four.

Si-Khrong Mu Yang

(Barbecued Spareribs)

INGREDIENTS :

2 1/2	lbs. spareribs	1/4	tsp. ground nutmeg
3	tbsp. light soy sauce	1/4	tsp. ground cinnamon
1	tsp. salt	1 1/2	tbsp. minced ginger
3	tbsp. whiskey	1	tsp. pepper

PREPARATION:

■ Cut the spareribs into pieces about 5 inches long and about 3 inches — or three ribs — wide.

■ Sprinkle the soy sauce and whiskey onto the spareribs so as to wet all surfaces. Mix the salt, nutmeg, cinnamon, ginger, and pepper together and then smear the mixture onto the ribs, covering them completely. Set aside to marinate for an hour.

■ Broil the spareribs over a slow charcoal fire until the meat is done and the outside is crisp.

■ Cut the ribs into 2 inch pieces and serve with cucumber, pineapple, spring onions and lettuce. Serve with sweet chilli sauce (see previous recipe).

■ Serves four.

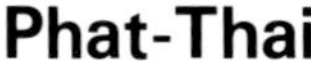

Phat-Thai

(Thai Fried Noodles)

INGREDIENTS :

7	oz. narrow rice noodles, soaked and drained
3	tbsp. cooking oil
1	tbsp. chopped garlic
1	egg
4	tbsp. diced firm yellow beancurd
3	oz. prawns, shelled and deveined
1/2	tbsp. pickled Chinese radish
3	tbsp. sugar
2	tbsp. fish sauce
4	tbsp. vinegar
1/2	tbsp. paprika
2	tbsp. chopped roasted peanuts
6	oz. bean sprouts
1/3	cup spring onions, cut into 1″ lengths
1/4	tsp. ground chilli
1	fresh lime, sliced

PREPARATION:

- In a large frying pan, heat oil over medium-high heat, sauté the garlic and pickled radish for 1 minute; then, add the egg and keep stirring. Add the prawns, beancurd and the noodles; then, season with sugar, fish sauce, vinegar, paprika and 1 tbsp. peanuts. Toss and cook for 10 minutes, until noodles turn soft. Then, add the spring onions, ground chilli and half of the bean sprouts, and remove from heat. Garnish with 1 tbsp. of chopped roasted peanuts.
- Serve with the remaining bean sprouts with the lime on the side.
- Serves two.

Sen Jan Phat Kung

(Stir-Fried Rice Noodles and Prawns)

INGREDIENTS:

1/2	lb. prawns shelled and deveined
1/2	cup sliced shallots
2	tbsp. sliced garlic
5	dried chillies, seeds removed, soaked in water
1/4	cup palm sugar
1/4	cup tamarind juice
1/4	cup fish sauce
1	oz. bean sprouts
4	oz. Chinese chives (see page 20)
1/4	cup cooking oil
2-3	limes
10	oz. dried narrow rice noodles (Chanthaburi noodles), soaked about 5 minutes in water

PREPARATION:

■ Slice the dried chillies. Place the chillies and salt in a mortar and pound until fine. Add the garlic, shallots and palm sugar. Pound until fine and well mixed.

■ Heat the oil in a wok. When the oil is hot, add the pounded chillie paste, stirring until well mixed.. Add the prawns. Stir frequently until done.

■ Add the noodles, tamarind juice and fish sauce. Stir for a few minutes. Add the bean sprouts and Chinese chives (cut into short lengths). Mix well and remove from heat.

■ Serve noodles on a bed of banana flowers, bean sprouts, and Chinese chives with lime wedges on the side.

■ Serves two to three

Khao Phat Mu Kung Sai Khai

(Fried Rice with Pork, Shrimp and Egg)

INGREDIENTS :

1 1/2	cups rice
5	oz. pork
5	oz. shrimp, shelled and deveined
2	eggs
1/4	cup cooking oil
1	onion
2	tbsp. catsup
1	tbsp. sugar
3	tbsp. light soy sauce
1	coriander plant
1	red chilli
2	cucumbers
6	spring onions
2	limes

PREPARATION:

- Steam the rice using 2 1/2 cups water for about 40 minutes. When the rice is done, rake it to separate the grains.
- Cut the pork into small pieces and marinate in 1 tbsp. light soy sauce for a few minutes.
- Cut the onion into slices about 1/5 inch thick.
- Heat the oil in a wok; when the oil is hot, fry the onions and then the pork, shrimp, catsup, sugar, and soy sauce. Sauté until the pork is done and then add the rice. Continue stirring the rice, scraping the bottom of the wok regularly to guard against sticking, until the desired degree of dryness is reached; then, remove the rice from the wok.
- Return the wok to the heat, add 1 tbsp. of oil, allow it to heat and then break the eggs into the wok. With the spatula, break, spread, and turn the eggs, and when done, cut into strips, remove from the wok, and mix with the fried rice.
- Peel the cucumbers and cut into discs. Slice the chilli into long shreds.
- Put the fried rice on a plate, sprinkle with chopped coriander and shreds of chilli, and serve with cucmber, spring onions, and wedges of lime.
- Serves four.

Khao Rat Na Kai

(Chicken in Sauce on Rice)

INGREDIENTS :

1 lb. rice
1 lb. chicken
4 oz. chicken livers
1 onion
3 oz. pineapple, cut into small pieces
3 oz. cherry tomatoes, halved
4 oz. Chinese mustard greens (phak kwangtung)
1 cup (4 oz.) spring onions cut into 1 inch lengths
2 coriander plants, roots removed
3 tbsp. light soy sauce
2 1/2 cup chicken stock
3 tbsp. tapioca flour mixed in 1/4 cup water
1 tsp. sugar
1 tbsp. chopped garlic
2 tbsp. cooking oil
1/2 tsp. pepper
3 chillies
1/4 cup vinegar
2 green bell peppers

PREPARATION:

- Wash the rice, divide into five portions, and place each in a steaming cup. Add 2/3 cup water to each cup and steam until done.
- Cut the chicken meat and livers into small slices and marinate in 1 tbsp. light soy sauce.
- Peel and wash onion, cut in half, then cut into thin slices.
- Heat oil in a wok, brown the garlic, then add the chicken meat and livers and fry until done. Add the onion slices. When cooked, add the mushrooms, mustard greens, and hot chicken stock. Add light soy sauce and sugar to taste and thicken with the tapioca flour in water. When boiling, taste and season as necessary, then add the spring onions and remove from heat.
- Invert the cups of steamed rice on serving plates and tap to remove rice. Spoon the hot Chicken sauce over the rice, decorate with shredded green bell peppers, sprinkle with pepper, and serve immediately.
- Serve with the chilli cut into thin rings soaked in vinegar.
- Serves five.

Khao Man Kai

(Chicken with Rice Cooked in Chicken Broth)

INGREDIENTS :

2	chicken breasts or thighs (1 lb.)
3	cups water .
1	tsp. salt
2	crushed coriander roots
1 1/2	cups rice
3	tbsp. cooking oil
10	slightly crushed garlic cloves
5	cucumbers (see page 21)
1	coriander plant, root removed

PREPARATION:

- Place the chicken in a pot with the 3 cups water, salt, and coriander roots and boil until the chicken is done. Skim off any froth, and use low heat to get a clear broth. Remove the chicken from the pot, debone it, and cut into thin slices. Strain the broth.
- Wash the rice, pour off water, and allow to stand a while.
- Heat the oil in a wok and add garlic. Before the garlic browns, add the rice and fry 3 minutes. Place the rice into a pot, add 2 1/2 cups chicken broth, and cook until the rice is done.
- Spoon the rice onto plates, arrange the chicken slices on top and garnish with coriander. Slice the cucumbers into 1/4 inch discs and put on the sides of the plates. Serve with fermented soybean sauce.

INGREDIENTS FOR FERMENTED SOYBEAN SAUCE :

3	tbsp. fermented soybeans
1	tsp. dark soy sauce
1	tbsp. vinegar
1	tsp. sugar
1	tbsp. mature ginger, well pounded
1	chilli, well pounded

PREPARATION:

- Strain the fermented soybeans and collect the liquid. Pound the solid portion thoroughly and mix with the liquid. Mix in the soy sauce, vinegar, sugar, ginger, and chilli. Spoon into small dishes.
- Serves three.

Khao Phat Kapi

(Stir-Fried Rice and Shrimp Paste)

INGREDIENTS :

3	cups cooked rice
1	cup thinly sliced pork
1	tbsp. shrimp paste
1	tbsp. water
1	tbsp. fish sauce
4	shallots sliced thin
1	tbsp. minced garlic
3	tbsp. fried dried shrimp
2	limes
1	tsp. sugar
1	cup cooking oil
1	egg
1	coriander plant, coarsely chopped
1	red chilli sliced thin
6	cucumbers (see page 21)

INGREDIENTS FOR SWEET PORK :

1/2	cup pork, thinly sliced
2	tbsp. palm sugar
1	tbsp. chopped garlic
1	tbsp. fish sauce
2	tsp. dark soy sauce
2	tbsp. cooking oil
1/4	cup water

PREPARATION:

- Fry the garlic in a wok. Add the pork, and when it is done, mix the water with the shrimp paste and add to the wok. Add the sugar and fish sauce and reduce the heat.
- Add the rice and stir with the spatula to mix well. When the rice is hot, add the shallots, mix thoroughly, and remove from the wok.
- Beat the egg. Place 1 tbsp. oil in a wok and heat. When the wok is hot, spread the oil, pour in the egg, and spread it in a thin layer over the wok. When set well, remove from the wok, roll up, and cut into thin slices.
- Spoon portions of the rice onto plates, add egg, sweet pork and dried shrimp, sprinkle with coriander and chilli, and serve with cucumber slices and wedges of lime.

PREPARATION:

- Mix the pork and the garlic. Fry the pork in the cooking oil until the pork is just done.
- Add the fish sauce, dark soy sauce and sugar, stirring regularly. Add the water. Cover the wok and simmer until the water is dried. Remove from heat.
- Serves three to four.

Khao Op Kun Chiang

(Chinese Sausage Steamed in Rice)

INGREDIENTS :

2	cups rice
2	Chinese sausages (kun chiang)
3 1/2	oz. lean pork
6	oz. small prawns
3	Shiitake mushrooms, soaked in water
2	tbsp. oyster sauce
2	tbsp. light soy sauce
10	cloves garlic, chopped
4	tbsp. cooking oil
1	tip of ginger root, diced

PREPARATION:

- Slice the sausage. Cut the pork into small thin strips. Shell and clean the prawns.
- After the mushrooms have absorbed water and filled out, cut them into thin slices. Save the water in which the mushrooms were soaked.
- Wash and drain the rice.
- Place the oil in a wok over medium heat. When it is hot, put in the garlic and ginger and fry, stirring long enough for the flavors to come out; then, add the sausage. When the sausage is hot and fragrant, add the pork, prawns, and mushrooms. Stir, adding the rice and then the oyster sauce and soy sauce. Work with the spatula until all the ingredients are thoroughly mixed; then, transfer the mixture to a pot.
- Add enough water to the water in which the mushrooms were soaked to obtain a total of three cups, add this to the pot, and then place the pot on the heat.
- Cooking time is about 30-35 minutes. Toward the end, cover the pot and reduce the heat. When the rice is done, remove from the heat and allow the rice to stand for a time in the covered pot. Spoon onto plates and serve with pineapple or fresh vegetables, such as cabbage and spring onions.
- Serves four.

Neua Tun

(Stewed Beef)

INGREDIENTS :

1	lb. beef shank
10	cups water
1	cm. length of cinnamon, broken into small pieces
1/2	inch length of galangal
3	coriander roots
2	tbsp. light soy sauce
1	tbsp. dark soy sauce
1/2	tsp. salt
1	bay leaf (krawan leaf)
2	celery plants(see page 20)
7	oz. lettuce, swamp cabbage, or bean sprouts
2	tbsp. fried garlic
1/2	tsp. ground black pepper
1	tbsp. chopped fresh coriander

PREPARATION:

- Wash the meat, cut into 1 inch cubes, place in pot.
- Add the water, cinnamon, galangal, coriander roots, light soy sauce, dark soy sauce, salt, and bay leaf.
- Heat to a boil, then cover, reduce heat, and simmer until the meat is tender. (If using an ordinary pot, this will be 3-4 hours. With a pressure cooker use only 2 cups of water and cook for 25 minutes, then remove from heat, allow to cool, open lid, and add 3 cups boiled water. Season to taste and bring to a boil once again).
- Blanch the vegetables, cut into 1 inch pieces and place on the bottom of the serving bowl. Pour the stewed beef on top of the vegetables, sprinkle with coarsely cut fresh coriander, celery, fried garlic and ground pepper. Serve with steamed rice or noodles.
- Serves four.

Khanom Jin Nam Ya

(Vermicelli and Fish Sauce)

INGREDIENTS FOR SPICE MIXTURE :

7	shallots, cut up coarsely
2	garlic gloves
2	tsp. sliced galangal
2	tbsp. sliced lemon grass
1	cup minced krachai
3	dried chillies, seeds removed
1	tsp. salt
1	tsp. shrimp paste
1	one-inch thick piece of salted fish, roasted
1	cup water

OTHER INGREDIENTS :

2	lbs. grated coconut or 5 cups coconut milk
1	meaty fish (1 lb.)
2-3	tbsp. fish sauce
2	hard boiled eggs, each peeled and cut into 5 sections
2	lbs. vermicelli
4	oz. yard-long beans, cut into short lengths and boiled a short time
4	oz. boiled swamp cabbage, cut into thin slices
4	oz. boiled bean sprouts
1	cup sweet basil leaves (maenglak)
1	chilli

ground dried chillies

PREPARATION:

- Place all the spice mixture ingredients in a pot and simmer over low heat until tender. Remove from heat, cool, place in mortar or blender and pound or blend to a fine paste.
- Add 2 1/2 cups warm water to the grated coconut and squeeze out 5 cups coconut milk. Skim off 1/2 cup coconut cream and set aside to add at the end.
- Wash and clean the fish, removing head and entrails, and boil until done in 1 cup water. Save the water in which the fish was boiled.
- Remove the meat from the fish, add to the blended spice mixture and blend thoroughly. Pour the mixture into a pot, mix in the coconut milk, and heat to boiling. Add the fish broth and fish sauce and simmer, stirring regularly to prevent sticking. When the sauce has thickened add the coconut cream and remove from the heat.
- Arrange the vermicelli, vegetables, and eggs on plates. Just before serving, spoon the hot sauce over the noodles.

Khanom Jin Nam Phrik

(Vermicelli and Prawn Sauce)

INGREDIENTS FOR SPICE MIXTURE :

2	tbsp. roasted shallots
2	tbsp. roasted garlic
1	tsp. roasted galangal
1	tbsp. chopped coriander root
1	dried small chillie

OTHER INGREDIENTS :

1	lb. grated coconut or 3 3/4 cups coconut milk
1	lb. prawns, shelled and deveined
2	oz. ground roasted shelled mungbeans
2	tbsp. chopped garlic
7	tbsp. ground dried chillies
1/4	cup cooking oil
6	tbsp. fish sauce
6	tbsp. palm sugar
6	tbsp. lemon juice
1	lb. vermicelli
2	cups chopped green apple or raw papaya
2	cups sliced swamp cabbage or cabbage

PREPARATION:

- Pound the roasted garlic, shallots, galangal, coriander root and dried chillies in a mortar until well ground and thoroughly mixed.
- Add 2 1/2 cups warm water to the grated coconut and squeeze out 3 3/4 cups coconut milk. Skim off 1 cup coconut cream. Place coconut cream in a pot and heat until some oil surfaces, remove from heat and set aside.
- Heat 1 cup of the remaining coconut milk and 1 cup of water to boiling, add the prawns. When the prawns are done, remove them from the pot, place them in a mortar, and pound well.
- Add the remaining 1 3/4 cups of coconut milk to the pot in which the prawns were cooked. Add, a little at a time and stirring after each addition, the ground spice mixture along with the pounded prawns. Then, mix in the mungbeans and add the fish sauce, palm sugar, and lime juice to give the sauce a sour, sweet, and salty taste. Remove the pot from the heat.
- Sauté the chopped garlic in the cooking oil. When it begins to brown, remove the garlic from the oil, put in ground chilli and reduce the heat.
- When the oil has taken on a red color, transfer it to the pot containing the sauce, add the coconut milk set aside earlier, and sprinkle with the sauteéd garlic.
- To serve, place four coils of vermicelli on each plate, add about 2 tbsp. of shredded papaya or apple and about 2 tbsp. of vegetable, and then spoon on about 1/2 cup of the sauce.

Ta-Ko
(Thai-Style Tapioca)

INGREDIENTS :

2 1/2	cups small tapioca pearls
3 1/4	cups water
1	cup sugar

TOPPING :

2	cups coconut milk
2	tsp. sugar
1/4	cup rice flour
1	tsp. salt

PREPARATION:

- Wash and drain the tapioca pearls; transfer to a pot, add the sugar and water; boil about 20 minutes until done.
- Spoon the tapioca into individual small bowls and top with a few spoonfuls of the coconut milk mixture.

TOPPING:

- Mix together the coconut milk, salt, sugar and rice flour in another pot, place over medium-low heat and cook until the mixture thickens.
- Serves four.

Khanom Mo Kaeng Pheuak

(Taro Coconut Custard)

INGREDIENTS :

1 1/2	cups mashed boiled taro
1 1/4	cups coconut milk
5	eggs, slightly beaten
1	tbsp. all-purpose flour
1/2	tsp. salt
1 1/4	cups palm sugar
1	tbsp. fried, thinly sliced shallot

PREPARATION:

- In a mixing bowl, mix the coconut milk, flour and sugar well. Set aside.
- In a separate bowl, mix the taro, eggs, and salt; beat until smooth.
- Combine both mixtures in a pot and cook over medium heat for 5 minutes, then remove from heat.
- Put this mixture in separate serving bowls, and bake in oven at 350 °F. for 35 minutes, or until golden brown on top. Garnish with the fried shallots.
- Serves four.

Thua Khiao Tom Nam Tan

(Mungbeans in Syrup)

INGREDIENTS :

1	cup mungbeans
1	cup light brown sugar
5	cups water

PREPARATION:

- Soak the mungbeans overnight or at least three hours, and then drain.
- Boil the mungbeans in the 5 cups water until tender and then add the sugar. When the sugar has dissolved completely and the syrup has returned to a strong boil, remove from the heat.
- Serves four.

Fak Thong Kaeng Buat

(Pumpkin in Coconut Cream)

INGREDIENTS :

2	lbs. pumpkin
4	cups coconut milk
1	cup sugar
1/2	tsp. salt
1	cup water

PREPARATION:

- Wash the skin of the pumpkin clean. Remove some, but not all, of the skin; the outer surface need not be completely smooth. Remove the seeds and membrane from the inside and cut the flesh into uniform pieces about one-half inch thick.
- Take 1 cup of the coconut milk, mix it with the sugar, salt, and the 1 cup water, heat to boiling, add the pumpkin, and continue cooking. When the pumpkin is tender, add the remaining coconut milk, bring to a boil once again, and remove from the heat. Serve in small bowls.
- Serves four.

Khao Phot Piak

(Corn Pudding with Coconut Cream)

INGREDIENTS :

3	cups sliced kernels of corn	4	tbsp. tapioca flour or corn flour
2	cups water	1	cup coconut milk
1	cup sugar	1/2	tsp. salt.

PREPARATION:

- Heat the water to boiling, add the corn, and boil, stirring constantly, until tender (five to ten minutes).
- Add the sugar and the flour, stirring all the while, continue cooking. When smooth, remove from the heat.
- Add salt to the coconut milk, bring to a boil, and then remove from the heat.
- Place a portion of the corn pudding into individual dessert dishes and top with the coconut milk.
- Serves four.

Kluai Buat Chi

(Bananas in Coconut Cream)

INGREDIENTS :

10	ripe Nam Wa variety bananas (see page 17)
1/2	cup coconut cream
3	cups coconut milk
1	cup sugar
1	tsp. salt

PREPARATION:

- Peel the bananas and cut into quarters.
- Place the coconut milk in a pot and heat to boiling. Add the bananas and cook over a medium heat until tender; then, add the sugar and salt; stir until dissolved.
- Add the coconut cream, spoon into bowls, and serve.

  Khai-variety bananas may also be used.

  If the bananas are very ripe, reduce the amount of sugar used. If the bananas are not yet fully ripe, they may not be sweet and may have a certain astringency. If so, first boil the bananas in plain water. Remove them from the water, and then proceed as in the above recipe except that the sugar should be dissolved in the coconut milk before the bananas are added. This will reduce the astringency and give the bananas and coconut cream a more appetizing appearance.

- Serves four to five.

Man Tom Nam Tan
(Sweet Potatoes in Syrup)

INGREDIENTS :

1	lb. sweet potatoes
1	cup sugar
4-5	slices mature ginger

PREPARATION:

■ Peel the sweet potatoes, wash well, and slice them across into discs about one inch thick. Cut each disc into 4-6 wedges and soak in water.

■ Bring 4 cups water to a boil, add the sweet potato. When the pot comes to a boil once again, add the ginger and cook until the potato is tender. Then, add the sugar and leave on the heat until all the sugar has dissolved and the pot has returned to a good boil.

■ Serves four.

Man Cheuam
(Candied Sweet Potato)

INGREDIENTS :

1	lb. large sweet potatoes
1 1/2	cups sugar
2	cups water
1 1/2	cups limewater

PREPARATION:

■ Wash the sweet potatoes well and peel them. Cut them into pieces about 3/4-inch thick. (If the sweet potatoes are small, slice them lengthwise; if large, slice across into discs.) Soak the sweet potato in limewater about half an hour and then wash in clean water before candying.

■ Place 2 cups water in a sauce pan or a wok and heat. When the water is hot, add the sugar and stir until it dissolves. If necessary, filter the solution to remove foreign matter.

■ Now bring the sugar solution to a boil in a wok. Allow to boil about five minutes and then add the sweet potatoes. The sweet potatoes need not be stirred often; they should, however, be turned from time to time. Reduce the heat as the syrup thickens and contiue cooking until the syrup penetrates the potato completely.

■ Serves four.

Kluai Khaek

(Fried Bananas)

INGREDIENTS :

3/4	cup rice flour
1/4	cup tapioca flour
2	tbsp. sugar
1	tsp. salt
1/2	cup grated coconut
1-1 1/4	cups water
10	Nam Wa variety bananas
3	cups cooking oil

The bananas should be just ripening : still green but beginning to turn yellow. Fried sweet potato and fried taro may also be made following this recipe.

PREPARATION:

- Mix the rice and tapioca flours, sugar, salt, and grated coconut; then, adding water a little at a time, knead the ingredients until thoroughly mixed and of the consistency of a fairly thick batter.
- Peel the bananas and cut each one lengthwise into three or four slices.
- Place the slices in the batter so that they are completely coated with it.
- Place the oil in a deep wok over high heat. When the oil is hot, fry the bananas to a golden brown; then, remove from the oil and drain.

Khao Tom Mat

(Banana and Glutinous Rice Steamed in Banana Leaf)

INGREDIENTS :

banana leaf

1	cup black beans, boiled until soft
1	lb. glutinous rice (soaked for 30 minutes)
14	oz. grated coconut or 2 cups coconut milk
1/2	cup sugar
2	tbsp. salt
10	bananas (Nam Wa variety) (see page 17)

PREPARATION:

- Wash and drain the rice.
- Mix 1 cup warm water with the coconut and squeeze out 2 cups coconut milk.
- Dissolve the sugar and salt in the coconut milk and strain into a pan, add the rice, then cook over low heat with constant stirring until mixture is dry.
- Peel the bananas and slice in half lengthwixse.
- Tear the banana leaf from edge to midrib into pieces 7-8 inches wide and place together in pairs so the midrib side of one is opposite that of the other. Put some rice on the leaf, place a half banana on the rice, cover the banana with more rice, press several black beans into the rice, then wrap up in the leaf. If desired, tie the packet; then, steam for 40-45 minutes.

  If the rice has not been soaked, the packets must be tied securely and boiled for 1 hour.

Aisa-khrim Ka-thi

(Coconut Milk Ice Cream)

INGREDIENTS :

3 1/2	cups coconut milk
1	cup sugar
1/2	cup water

PREPARATION:

- Place the sugar and water in a pot and heat until the sugar dissolves. If necessary, filter the solution through cheesecloth to remove any foreign matter and then return to the heat. Continue heating to obtain a syrup thick enough to stick to a wooden paddle; then, remove from the heat.
- When the syrup has cooled somewhat but is still warm, add the coconut milk and stir to mix well.
- Pour the solution into an ice cream freezer and crank about 45 minutes, or until stiff. Coconut milk ice cream must be kept cold because it melts rapidly.
- To serve, scoop the ice cream into a dessert dish. You may sprinkle with 1 tbsp. roasted peanuts.

  For variety, try adding shreds of ripe jackfruit or young coconut meat before putting the mixture into the ice cream freezer.
- Note: freshly squeezed coconut milk will make the best ice cream. (See page 17)
- Serves six.

Kafae Yen or Cha Yen

(Thai-Style Iced Coffee or Tea)

INGREDIENTS :

2 tbsp. ground coffee or powdered Thai tea leaves
1 1/2 cups boiling water
4 tbsp. sugar
1/4 cup unsweetened condensed milk
crushed ice or ice cubes

PREPARATION:

- Place ground coffee or powered tea leaves in a cloth bag.
- Place bag in a mug and pour the boiling water into the bag. Allow to steep a few moments, lift bag to a second mug, pour contents of the first mug into the bag, and repeat until desired strength is reacher.
- Remove bag, add sugar and milk, stir until dissolved, and pour into ice-filled glasses.
- Serves two.

INDEX

A

APPETIZERS

B

BEEF

C

CHICKEN

CRAB

CURRY

CURRY PASTE

D

DRINKS

DUCK

F

FISH

L

LOBSTER

N

NOODLES

P

PORK

PRAWNS

R

RICE

S

STIR FRIED

SUN DRIED

SWEETS

T

TAMARIND

V

VEGETABLE

Books from Snow Lion Graphics/SLG Books

Cook Books	Price
The Elegant Taste of Thailand 0-943389-23-2	$22.00
The Vegetarian Taste of Thailand 0-943389-13-5	$22.00
Luba Gurdjieff: A Memoir with Recipes 0-943389-22-4	$15.95
Still Eatin' It: A New Dana Crumb Cook Book 0-943389-18-6	$18.00

Pop Culture	
Freehand: The Art of Stanley Mouse	
Paperback 0-943389-11-9	$24.95
Hardback 0-943389-12-7	$39.95
Limited Deluxe (bound & boxed in Blue suede)0--943389-24-0	$250.00
Photopass 0-943389-17-8	$15.00
Big Yum Yum Book 0-943389-19-4	$20.00
Don't You Want Somebody to Love 943389-08-9	$15.95
The Droll Troll 0-943389-15-1	$10.00
Still Eatin' It: A New Dana Crumb Cook Book 0-943389-18-6	$18.00

Tibet	
Mipam 0-961706-0-0	$12.95
The Unveiling of Lhasa	
Paperback 0-9617066-1-9	$12.95
Hardback 0-9617066-2-7	$19.95
Lands of the Thunderbolt	
Paperback 0-9617066-6-X	$12.95
Hardback 0-9617066-7-8	$19.95
Wind Between the Worlds, British Title: Captured in Tibet	
Paperback 0-9617066-8-6	$12.95
Hardback 0-9617066-9-4	$19.95
A Tibetan on Tibet 0-943389-02-X	$12.95
Healing Image: The Great Black One 0-943389-06-2	$14.95

Order Form

Mail this form to:
Snow Lion Graphics/SLG Books
P.O. Box 9465
Berkeley, CA 94709
or Fax it to: 1-510-525-2632
Phone orders (orders only) 1-800-603-9903

Name ______________________________

Address ______________________________

City ____________ State ____________ Zip ____________

Daytime Phone ______________________________

Qty	Title	Price
____	______________________________	________
____	______________________________	________
____	______________________________	________
____	______________________________	________
____	______________________________	________
____	______________________________	________
____	______________________________	________
	Subtotal	________
	8.25 tax (Ca only)	________
	Shipping & Handling	________
	(see chart)	________
	TOTAL	________

Shipping & Handling for individual orders

United States:

USPS Book Rate $2.50 for first item; $1.00 for each additional item
USPS Priority Rate $3.00 for first item; $1.50 for each additional item
UPS: $5.00 for first item; $1.00 for each additional item

Foreign:

USPS Book Rate $5.00 for first item; $2.00 for each additional item
For Foreign Air Mail and deluxe item shipping cost contact Publisher.